"The cutting edge of Christian evangelism today is blunted, the bond of love between many Christian leaders severely weakened, and the peace of mind of thoughtful individuals is destroyed by what seems to be a contradiction of faith and science over the age of the physical universe. Simply put, it is suggested that you cannot be a Christian unless you reject the teachings of current science about the origin of the earth. In a spirit of peace, and with complete mastery of the relevant biblical, historical and scientific data, Hugh Ross effectively deals with all points of tension in this painful situation. His careful, undogmatic explorations will be a path to liberations for those troubled by them. It is especially important that young people of high school and university age, and all those in positions of leadership, give a prayerful and thoughtful reading to this book. As one who daily deals with the destructive consequences of this conflict on young people in the universities, I plead with all in charge of youth groups to use *Creation and Time* intensely with their students."

Dallas Willard
Professor of Philosophy
University of Southern California

"As a scientist who was taught and believed for many years that recent creation was the only option available for a Bible believing Christian, I can only wish that I had had available *Creation and Time* twenty-five years ago. Dr. Ross has very carefully and fairly summarized all of the arguments for a recent creation and a progressive creation, leaving God fully in charge and immediately responsible for each. His painstaking presentation of the relevant data and insightful analysis lead the reader unmistakably to the conclusion that progressive creation better satisfies both the biblical and the scientific data. This is a message the evangelical church needs to hear, lest the remarkably testimony of modern science to the existence of God be obscured in unnecessary arguments about the age of the universe."

Brent Stucker, Ph.D. Student
Mechanical Engineering Department
Texas A&M University

"*Creation and* [...] needed book [...] cise the Christ[...] exhibited in controversies of this sort. Its irenic and evidential style, with special emphasis on the major advances supplied by the field of astrophysics, needs to be heard by all serious inquirers into the matters of cosmic origins. It is our desire that his concluding proposal will be acted on in the near future, for it is desperately needed in the evangelical community."

Walter C. Kaiser, Jr.
Colman M. Mockler Distinguished Professor of Old Testament
Gordon-Conwell Theological Seminary

"Hugh Ross is a true friend of all Christians who hold to the inerrancy and full and final authority of the Bible. Furthermore, in *Creation and Time*, he excellently preserves the literal interpretation of Scripture by carefully handling both the figurative and non-figurative genre.

"Evangelical Christianity is hurtfully divided over the issue of the age of the earth at a time when they ought to be focusing on God as the Creator in contrast to the secular focus of naturalism and materialism as ultimate answers to reality. Dr. Ross has presented a credible reconciliation of the interpretation of the revelation of God in nature and in Scripture. He has shown that the words of the Bible and the facts of nature form a perfectly harmonious revelation."

Earl Radmacher, Th.D.
Chancellor, Western Seminary

"*Creation and Time* is a compelling contribution to removing the age issue as a barrier to intellectuals coming to faith in Christ. Those of us who minister in the university have benefited immensely from Dr. Ross's previous work. We have waited with anticipation for *Creation and Time*, expecting careful theology and good science. Dr. Ross has not disappointed us."

Stan Oakes, Director
Christian Leadership Ministries
(Faculty Ministry of Campus Crusade for Christ)

"A fear often expressed by Bible believing Christians is whether they can trust scientists who claim to believe but seem willing to compromise important biblical truth in order to achieve harmony with science. As a scientist who is an evangelical Christian with strong fundamentalist roots and leanings, I am not only excited with the strong biblical case that Dr. Ross has put together in support of long creation days, I am also delighted to testify from personal knowledge to his unswerving commitment to the inerrancy and infallibility of God's Word."

David H. Rogstad, Ph.D., Physicist
Caltech Jet Propulsion Laboratory

"Echoing Philip Abelard, Hugh Ross writes, "When science appears to be in conflict with theology, we have no reason to reject either the facts of nature or the Bible's words. Rather we have reason to re-examine our interpretation of these facts and words because sound science and sound biblical exegesis will always be in harmony." This should be a fundamental addition to the seven standard rules of theological hermeneutics and should be taught in every church and in every school to stop the unwarranted war between science and religion."

Allan Sandage, Astronomer
Recipient of the Crafoord Prize

"Dr. Ross compassionately explains the historical miscues that have caused many very sincere Christians to feel obligated, in their deep loyalty to Scripture to adopt an interpretation of recent creation. Then with a loyalty to Scripture manifestly as strong, he corrects the miscues and unveils a synthesis of biblical truth and scientific observation that is both mature and compelling."

Don Richardson, author of *Peace Child*
and *Eternity in Their Heart*

"Hugh Ross's approach combines scientific, historical, biblical, and theological reflection in a manner that makes a compelling case for and effective evangelistic approach to the scientific community."

Jim Berney, General Director
Inter-Varsity Christian Fellowship
of Canada

"*Creation and Time* is a welcome addition to the discussion in the Christian community on the Bible and science. Dr. Ross holds to the inerrancy of Scripture, the doctrine of divine creation, and also the concept of an ancient universe.

"In recent years there has been a rather militant stance by many Christians that inerrancy and a young earth must go together, and to hold otherwise is tantamount to heresy, or at least extreme compromise. However, for years Christians who have held to inerrancy have allowed for differences of interpretation concerning the age of the universe. The Scofield Bible presented the gap theory; others held a day-age theory; others held to twenty-four-hour creation and an earth 6,000 years old; others held to genealogical gaps that might allow for the earth to be 20,000 years old; still others presented various views seeking to reconcile the Bible and science. The recent stance insisting on a young universe as the only orthodox possibility has led to unnecessary negative results: the loss of the creationist's case in the courts of the United States; an unnecessary stumbling block to the gospel for many who would otherwise be open to Christianity; a lack of openness to discuss differences of interpretation of both the Bible and science between believers; a reputation for closed-mindedness on the part of Christians toward science. Many young-earth creationists assert that God created the universe with an apparent age and history — the fossils in place would seek to determine which doctrines concerning creation are essential to Christian faith and which are not. He sees this as a set that would not condemn those holding a young-earth view, but would allow room for discussion of hard issues and would open the door of the gospel to the scientific community. This is an excellent suggestion, which I hope comes to pass.

"Whether you hold to an ancient earth or a young earth, *Creation and Time* is an important book for you to read."

Ted Martin, Th.D.
Director of Academic Affairs
International School of Theology
Campus Crusade for Christ

CREATION AND TIME

A BIBLICAL AND SCIENTIFIC PERSPECTIVE ON THE CREATION-DATE CONTROVERSY

DR. HUGH ROSS

NAVPRESS ◐
BRINGING TRUTH TO LIFE
NavPress Publishing Group
P.O. Box 35001, Colorado Springs, Colorado 80935

The Navigators is an international Christian organization. Jesus Christ gave His followers the Great
Commission to go and make disciples (Matthew
28:19). The aim of The Navigators is to help fulfill
that commission by multiplying laborers for Christ in
every nation.

NavPress is the publishing ministry of The Navigators. NavPress publications are tools to help
Christians grow. Although publications alone cannot
make disciples or change lives, they can help believers learn biblical discipleship, and apply what they
learn to their lives and ministries.

Library of Congress Catalog Card Number:
94-4308
ISBN 08910-97767

Cover illustration: Steve Dininno

Ross, Hugh (Hugh Norman), 1945-
    Creation and time : a biblical and
scientific perspective on the creation-date
controversy / by Hugh Ross.
        p.   cm.
    Includes bibliographical references and
indexes.
    ISBN 0-89109-776-7
    1. Creationism. 2. Biblical cosmology.
3. Bible and science. I. Title.
BS652.R67   1994
231.7'65—dc20   94-4308
                                       CIP

Printed in the United States of America

Contents

Acknowledgments

I cannot imagine a more supportive, helpful, and dedicated publishing team to work with than the NavPress crew. Steve Webb, John Eames, Debby Weaver, and all the rest have carefully guided each stage of this project, consistently demonstrating the Christlike character that to me typifies the Navigators ministry. Many thanks, also, to Dr. Jerry White and Denny Repko for their enthusiastic backing.

Only those who read the first draft can know how significantly this book benefited from suggestions and revisions offered by Steve Scheele, John Wiester, and Drs. Robert Bowman, Jr., Walter Bradley, David Carta, Sam Conner, Norm Geisler, Ted Martin, Alex Metherell, John Rea, David Rogstad, Dallas Willard, and Ralph Winter. Some of these individuals provided valuable research materials, and Mal Scharer hunted down additional references.

Janet Kobobel, director of publications for Reasons To Believe, contributed significantly to the book's readability. At the same time she kept me on schedule and maintained communications with NavPress and all the others involved—no small assignment.

Special thanks to my wife, Kathy, for her constructive critique and skillful rewriting of many sections, including chapter beginnings and endings. Over the past several years she has spent countless hours discussing with me the points of this book, helping me to think through them and communicate more clearly.

Last, but not least, Kathy Duerksen and Patty Bradbury deserve thanks for their attention to our sons, Joel and David, while we pressed hard to meet writing deadlines.

Introduction

Nearly half the adults in the United States believe that God created the universe within the last 10,000 years.[1,2] What reason do they give? "The Bible says so."

Meanwhile, more than 99 percent of America's practicing scientists view this idea as more far-fetched than the hypothesis that the earth is flat. Their reason? "The scientific record says so."

On no other issue has such a large segment of the American populace been in such direct opposition to the scientific community. On no other issue have the words of the Bible been pitted so sharply against the facts of nature.

Can science be trusted? Is the Bible flawed? Can that many Americans be wrong? Are scientists involved in a grand conspiracy to hide the facts from the public? Is there any hope of reconciliation?

In the following pages you will read my responses to all these questions, and most importantly, to the last one. I am convinced there *is* hope for reconciliation, a reconciliation that requires no compromise from either the biblical or the scientific side of the issue.

CHAPTER ONE

What's All the Fuss About?

For the past two hundred years the scientific and religious worlds have thundered at each other in a series of battles over God. Traditionally, the conflict has focused on these key questions:

- Does God exist?
- If He does, is He the God of the Bible?
- If He is the God of the Bible, how involved was He in forming the universe, the earth, the first life-form, subsequent life, and the human race?
- Is the Bible free of contradiction and error?

In the past thirty years, however, the debate has veered away from these core issues. Now the battle line has been drawn over a peripheral point—the age of the universe and of the earth.

Ours is the first generation that has witnessed the measuring of the universe, including its date of birth. In demarking the universe, astronomers in many respects are measuring the creation. In measuring the creation, they are determining several of the characteristics of the Creator, even certain aspects of His personality. This scientifically revealed Creator uniquely and decisively matches the character and characteristics of the biblically revealed God.[1]

Ironically, this exciting news is being ignored or rejected less by opponents of Christianity than by many Christians. Why? Because it threatens belief in a recent creation date for the universe.

This belief in a recently created universe has innoculated a large segment of secular society from taking seriously the call to faith in Christ. Worse yet, the courts in North America have come to perceive age as *the* central issue. Thus a pretext has been provided—the "Christian dogma" of a thousands-of-years-old universe and earth—for discounting the credibility of the Bible and for removing "religious notions" from public education and the public arena.

The creation date for the universe also has divided the Christian community into hostile camps. Often young-universe and old-universe creationists focus more energy on defending their respective positions than on reaching out to nonbelievers.

Meanwhile, an even larger segment of the Christian community hovers on the sidelines. Lacking the theological and scientific tools to resolve the issue for themselves, they remain distressed and confused. In the midst of this confusion, many long for simplicity, for a universe not so mind-boggling, vast and complex, and for answers untainted by the presumed corruption of secular research.

In their bewilderment and longing, many Christians react by refusing to support organizations that use science as a tool for reaching others for Christ, and they refuse to use science in their sharing of the gospel with nonChristians. Thus, not only does the faith of these Christians remain unstrengthened by scientific evidences, but also many secularists who need solid evidence to resolve their doubts remain untouched by the claims of Christ. Further, such secularists perceive evangelical Christians as anti-intellectuals, as individuals who "park their brains at the front door of the church."

What the Fuss Is *Not* About

Many Christians fear that by believing in a universe and an earth that is billions of years old they must accept a millions-of-years-old history for the human species. They see in a millions-of-years-old human species an implied denial of Adam and Eve as literal historical persons from whom the human race is descended.

Years ago at a conference on the Genesis creation accounts I shared the platform with three old-earth creationists and one young-earth creationist.[2] The young-earth creationist told the audience that in over twenty years of public speaking he had never met an old-earth creationist who believed we are all descended from an original human pair, specially created by God just thousands of years ago. He challenged the four of us to tell the audience exactly what we believed about Adam and Eve.

To everyone's surprise, all the old-earthers — despite some differences among us in our interpretation of Genesis — expressed belief in our direct descent from Adam and Eve, specially created by God several thousand years ago and unique among all God's creatures on Earth in possessing spirit capacities.

The troubling issue is not the historicity or the recency of Adam and Eve but rather the identity and historicity of the so-called human-like species before them. For more details, biblical and scientific, on the origin of humankind and the origin and extinction of the bipedal primates that preceded God's creation of human beings see chapter 13, pages 134-138.

A Needless Controversy

Few Christians comprehend just how destructive the age issue has become. The sad irony is that age need not even be an issue. But because it is, numbers of nonChristians turn away from the Christian message.

The three creation accounts of the Bible (Genesis 1, Genesis 2, and Psalm 104) emphasize most strongly the *who* of creation. To a significant degree they explain the *how* of creation. And to a much lesser degree they discuss the *when* of creation.

Given that the Bible teaches centrally about the steps men and women may take to form a relationship with their Creator, this order of emphasis is entirely appropriate. Misidentifying God or His key attributes could destroy the possibility of a person's relationship with Him. Misunderstanding God's strengths, capacities, and past works can impair the success of such a relationship. But misidentifying the timing of God's past works in the cosmos has little or no bearing on that relationship. Nor does it bear upon the Bible's authority. It appears ill-advised, then, to make an issue out of such a trivial doctrinal point.

Many Christians claim the Bible can only be interpreted as teaching that all creation took place in six, twenty-four-hour days—about 10,000 years (10^4 years) ago. Others say the text allows ample room, with no compromise of inerrancy, for a birth date of the cosmos of about 10,000,000,000 years (10^{10} years) ago.

Meanwhile, nontheists are being pushed by the evidence to concede that the age of the universe must exceed $10^{100,000,000,000}$ years for life to have self-assembled by natural processes. (See chapter 6, pages 53-72, for further discussion and a list of references to research, both by theists and nontheists, for this extreme age requirement.) Thus believers in the Creator are separated from unbelievers by a hundred-billion zeros in the index while young-universe creationists differ from old-universe creationists by only six zeros. For creationists to make an issue of such a relatively trivial difference seems both impolitic and unnecessary.

The emotionalism associated with the young- versus old-universe debate also is unnecessary. Science is an attempt to interpret the facts of nature. Christian theology is an attempt to interpret the words of the Bible. Since, according to that theology, God created the universe and is also responsible for the words of the Bible, and since He does not lie or deceive, there can be no contradiction between the words of the Bible and the facts of nature. Any conflict between science and Christian theology must be attributed to human misinterpretation. Such conflicts should be viewed with neither fear for the integrity of the Bible nor outrage against science, but rather should be accepted for the time being as indications that further research is needed. The Christian expectation is that such research will lead to greater understanding of both science and theology and to an eventual reconciliation that will uphold both the Bible and the data from nature.

Historically, such investigations have not only borne fruit in bringing warring parties to peace but also in providing new tools for leading people to Christ. With a desire for this fruit, I have written these pages, and I hope it is with this same desire that these pages will be read.

Personal Encounter

I came to Christ through a two-year personal study of the Bible. By the end of that study, I was convinced the Bible was free of contradiction and error doctrinally, historically, and scientifically. But, in the vicinity of my Canadian universities, I could not find a church or Christian group that shared all of my convictions. In coming to the United States, I found many who did, and I was overjoyed. Some showed great interest in my testimony and in the personal study that led me to give my life to Christ. Within a couple of years, I was invited to speak on science and the Bible at a Christian conference.

After my first message, a group of angry men headed my way. One was waving my booklet *What Is Christianity?*[3] in my face. He told me he was convinced no one but a genuine Christian could possibly write such words. But, he said when he next read my booklet, *Genesis One: A Scientific Perspective*,[4] he was forced to change his mind. Since that booklet implied the universe was billions of years old, he concluded I could not possibly be a Bible-believing Christian.

That was my first exposure to the flames of the controversy. I had offended those dozen men by failing even to mention the time-scale "problem" in my talk. Yet, up to that time, I was unaware such a problem existed.

Poisoning the Wells

Secularists are delighted that a majority of evangelical Christians believe in a young universe and a young earth. They are confident that they can exploit such a belief to win court cases related to teaching about creation in public institutions. Of greater importance, they believe that by discrediting Genesis, they can demonstrate a flawed Bible. Thus they can use this "faulty creation message" to discredit Christ's deity, the inerrancy of Scripture, the sanctity of life, the second coming, doctrines on heaven and hell, etc. After all, many Bible authors and Jesus Himself strongly endorsed the message of the Genesis creation account. If they could be so wrong on creation, what basis is there to believe anything else they declared?

An example of this line of reasoning is articulated in the book *Steve Allen on the Bible, Religion, and Morality*:

> The fundamentalist argument against the scientific assertion of the great age of our planet—to the effect that God created the earth only about 6000 years ago, including fossils embedded in rocks—is unworthy of serious discussion. . . . It is now recognized by every intelligent and informed person that the two [Genesis and science] cannot be reconciled. . . . Nor should we be guilty of the error of assuming that the problem relates only to Genesis. It touches the New Testament as well.[5]

Many secularists use the age of the universe to marginalize, patronize, and abuse the Christian community. They marginalize—that is, minimize and isolate—by consistently equating all Christians with young-universe creationists.

The term *creationist,* for example, is rarely qualified, even though one can be a creationist without also adhering to the young-universe view.

They patronize with such statements as this: "If you are a creationist, the Bible — not nature — dictates what you believe."[6] "The spurious stories in Genesis are simply absurd. Yet, they do represent a conceptual framework from the undisciplined imagination of a prescientific age."[7] "The biblical story of creation has great poetic beauty and meta-phorical power."[8] They patronize by exhorting high school science teachers to forbid classroom discussion about creation and to redirect students to discuss such issues "outside the domain of science" with their families and clergy.[9]

They abuse in their name-calling. Michael Ruse's oft-quoted railing against creationists is a prime example:

> There are degrees of being wrong. The Creationists are at the bottom of the scale. They pull every trick in the book to justify their position. Indeed, at times they verge right over into the downright dishonest. . . . Their arguments are rotten, through and through.[10]

Enemies of the Faith

Obviously these attacks have had an unfavorable impact on the Christian community. Small wonder so many Christians look fearfully, suspiciously, or bitterly at scientists and treat science as a hostile enemy of the faith.

Sadly, many Christians who are scientists by profession or hobby have been blasted by their brothers in the crossfire. Christians who believe that the Bible is true and that the universe and the earth are as old as the stars and rocks reveal are called "compromisers," whose lives and work "do not lead to soul-winning or spiritual growth, but to apostasy."[11] Lists of these apostates have been published: Calvin College geologist, Davis Young; Pattle Pun and all his science faculty colleagues at Wheaton College; most of the authors and officers of the American Scientific Affiliation; former young-universe creationist, Dan Wonderly; Alan Hayward; Charles Hummel; Howard Van Til; and Hugh Ross. (Yes, my name shows up on the lists, too.)

Russell Akridge, addressing the 1982 Annual Creation Convention, berated astrophysicists and astronomers as "high priests of the decades-old cult [of the] Big Bang myth, [and as] persuasive speakers [who] have deceived an unsuspecting public."[12]

Apostasy and disinterest in evangelism are serious charges to hurl at specific evangelical leaders. Such words engender hostility rather than harmony. Similarly, accusing all of the world's astronomers and astrophysicists of cultism, promoting myths, and purposeful deception gives slight likelihood of winning many friends from those disciplines.

With so much gasoline on the flames, does any hope exist for a peaceful resolution? I believe so. I am persuaded that more than enough evidence is now available to resolve the issue. *No compromise* of integrity is required by either side, not by the scientist who trusts in the established facts of nature, nor by the Christian who upholds the inerrancy of God's written Word.

As a first step toward resolution, I believe it is essential to trace the historical growth and development of the creation-date controversy. The bitter acrimony I have just described did not happen overnight. Though the date for the creation has been debated since the birth of the Christian church, that debate was open and friendly for fifteen centuries. But, beginning some 350 years ago, friendly dialogue slowly degenerated into nasty polarization.

CHAPTER TWO

Interpretations
of Early Church Leaders

In deciding difficult doctrinal questions, Christians often turn to the writings of early pastors and apologists who gave shape to the emerging church. The historical position of the church carries significant weight in those crucial matters where we find unanimity, matters such as the deity of Jesus Christ. Even in matters where these leaders were divided, their perspective may still be helpful since typically they were operating from a different context and culture. The time frame for creation is one of those matters.

Many Christians have been taught that through the first seventeen centuries of the church, until the industrial revolution and the scientific age, there was general agreement on the six-twenty-four-hour-creation-days interpretation.[1-3] But that is not what the literature shows.

To avoid stacking the deck and special pleading, let's review a list of prominent names and make note of their views, regardless of which case they support. My purpose is to establish an overview of the range of interpretations.

First-Century Jewish Scholars

The earliest scholars to record their thoughts about the six days of creation were Jews in the first century AD—Philo (c 20 BC–AD 45) and Josephus (AD 37–103).

Philo expressed the notion that God created everything

instantaneously and that the six days were figurative, a metaphor for order and completeness:

> He [Moses] says that in six days the world was created,
> not that its Maker required a length of time for His
> work, for we must think of God as doing all things
> simultaneously, remembering that "all" includes with
> the commands which He issues the thought behind
> them. Six days are mentioned because for the things
> coming into existence there was need of order.[4]

Philo amplified his reasoning in a later work:

> It is quite foolish to think that the world was created in
> six days or in a space of time at all. Why? Because every
> period of time is a series of days and nights, and these
> can only be made such by the movement of the sun as it
> goes over and under the earth; but the sun is a part of
> heaven, so that time is confessedly more recent than the
> world. It would therefore be correct to say that the
> world was not made in time, but that time was formed
> by means of the world, for it was heaven's movement
> that was the index of the nature of time. When, then,
> Moses says, "He finished His work on the sixth day,"
> we must understand him to be adducing not a quantity
> of days, but a perfect number, namely six.[5]

Josephus, in writing a survey of the Genesis creation days, noted the need to explain the meaning of the expression "one day" and promised to offer an explanation,[6] but he never fulfilled his promise. His comments suggest that he did not find this expression either easy or straightforward to interpret.

Second-Century Christian Scholars
The earliest known Christian writings on the subject of the creation time frame date to the second century. Justin Martyr

(c AD 100–166) and Irenaeus (c AD 130–200) used Psalm 90:4 and 2 Peter 3:8 as the support for their view that the creation days were each a thousand years long.[7-8]

Describing the events of the sixth creation day, Irenaeus expresses the reason behind his interpretation:

> Thus, then, in the day they did eat, in the same did they die. . . . For it is said, "There was made in the evening, and there was made in the morning one day." Now in this same day that they did eat, in that also did they die. . . . On one and the same day on which they ate they also died (for it is one day of creation). . . .
>
> He (Adam) did not overstep the thousand years, but died within their limit . . . for since "a day of the Lord is as a thousand years," he did not overstep the thousand years, but died within them.[9]

Third-Century Christian Scholars

Hippolytus (c AD 170–236), of the late second and early third centuries, apparently wrote more extensively than others on the Genesis creation days, but most of these writings have been lost. We learn from the writings of Ambrose (c AD 340–397), however, that Hippolytus, like Irenaeus, interpreted the days as a thousand years each.

Clement of Alexandria (c AD 150–220) echoed Philo's belief that the Genesis creation days were not literal, twenty-four-hour days.[10,11] He claimed that the creation days communicated the order and priority of created things but not the time. As he understood it, creation could not take place in time since "time was born along with things which exist."[12]

Origen (c AD 185–254) taught that in approaching certain difficulties in Scripture we should seek a spiritual meaning, not always a literal one. In the six creation days of Genesis he saw just such a difficulty.[13-14]

He claims that time as we mark it did not exist until the fourth day. Hence, for him, at least the first three creation days could not possibly have been twenty-four-hour days:

> The text said that "there was evening and there was morning," it did not say: "the first day," but said, "one day." It is because there was not yet time before the world existed. But time begins to exist with the following days.[15]

> Now what man of intelligence will believe that the first, and the second, and the third day, and the evening and the morning existed without the sun, moon, and stars?[16]

Neither could the seventh day be twenty-four hours, according to Origen. He saw the six Genesis creation days as representing the time that men work on the earth (the period of human history) while the seventh day represents the time between the creation of the world and its extinction at the ascension of all the righteous:

> He [Celsus] knows nothing of the day of the Sabbath and rest of God, which follows the completion of the world's creation, and which lasts during the duration of the world, and in which all those will keep festival with God who have done all their works in their six days, and who, because they have omitted none of their duties will ascend to the contemplation (of Celestial things) and to the assembly of righteous and blessed beings.[17]

Writing later in the third century, Lactantius (c AD 250–325), Victorinus of Pettau, and Methodius of Olympus, all concurred with Justin Martyr's and Irenaeus' view of the creation days as thousand-year epochs.[18-20]

Augustine's Analysis
Among all the early leaders of the Christian church, no one penned a more extensive analysis of the creation days than Augustine (AD 354-430). In *The City of God*, Augustine wrote,

"As for these 'days,' it is difficult, perhaps impossible to think — let alone explain in words — what they mean."[21] In *The Literal Meaning of Genesis*, he added, "But at least we know that it [the Genesis creation day] is different from the ordinary day with which we are familiar."[22] Elsewhere in that book he made this comment:

> Seven days by our reckoning after the model of the days of creation, make up a week. By the passage of such weeks time rolls on, and in these weeks one day is constituted by the course of the sun from its rising to its setting; but we must bear in mind that these days indeed recall the days of creation, but without in any way being really similar to them.[23]

Augustine took the evenings and mornings of the Genesis creation days in a figurative sense. He concluded that the evening of each creation day referred to the occasion when the angels gazed down on the created things after they contemplated the Creator, and that the morning referred to the occasion when they rose up from their knowledge of the created things to praise the Creator.[24]

In *Confessions* Augustine notes that for the seventh day Genesis makes no mention of an evening and a morning. From this omission he deduced God sanctified the seventh day, making it an epoch extending onward into eternity.[25]

Other Fourth-Century Scholars

Eusebius, a bishop of Caesarea (c AD 260–340), between AD 314 and 316 wrote a lengthy apologetic work, *Preparation for the Gospel*, which he arranged into fifteen books. In books I–VI he attacked the creation doctrines of the Greeks, Romans, Phoenicians, Egyptians, and pagans. In book VII he devoted six pages to explaining the Genesis creation account. However, nowhere in all this discussion does Eusebius ever address the date for the creation of the universe or the earth or the length of the Genesis creation days. Evidently, he was aware, nonetheless, that the Hebrew word for day, *yôm*, could refer to a time scale longer than twenty-four hours since he quotes Genesis 2:4 thusly:

> This is the book of the generation of heaven and earth, in the *day* that God made the heaven and the earth, and all the things that are therein.[26] (emphasis added)

In book XI Eusebius again brings up the subject of the events of creation but neglects any mention of the timing or the time scale for the creation events, other than to state that there was a definite point of beginning and to quote Genesis 2:4 as he did in book VII.[27]

Basil (c AD 330–379), a bishop of Caesarea, wrote nine homilies on the first chapter of Genesis. He hints at the difficulty of discovering the date for the universe's creation:

> You may know the epoch when the formation of the world began, if, ascending into the past, you endeavour to discover the first day. You will thus find what was the first movement of time.[28]

In reference to the first Genesis creation day Basil poses the question, "Why does Scripture say 'one day' not 'the first day'?" His response:

> The beginning of time is called "one day" rather than "the first day," it is because Scripture wishes to establish its relationship with eternity. It was, in reality, fit and natural to call "one" the day whose character is to be one wholly separated and isolated from all the others. If Scripture speaks to us of many ages, saying everywhere, "age of age, and ages of ages," we do not see it enumerate them as first, second, and third. It follows that we are hereby shown not so much limits, ends, and succession of ages, as distinctions between various states and modes of action.[29]

In the remainder of his homilies on the first chapter of Genesis, Basil shifts attention away from the timing of creation to the actions of God's creating—that is, to the how and what of His creation.

Ambrose (c AD 340–397), a bishop of Milan, is the early church leader most frequently quoted as supporting the interpretation of the six Genesis creation days as a 144-hour period. Among early church leaders Ambrose holds the record, by far, for commentary on the six creation days. But in his 280-page homily on the six days of creation he devotes less than a page to the discussion of the length of the creation days. Even then, he does not make an explicit statement as to their length. He appears to imply, though, that the creation days are twenty-four-hour periods:

> Scripture established a law that twenty-four hours, including both day and night, should be given the name of day only, as if one were to say the length of one day is twenty-four hours in extent. . . .
> The nights in this reckoning are considered to be component parts of the days that are counted. Therefore, just as there is a single revolution of time, so there is but one day.[30]

However, in the following sentence Ambrose—perhaps thinking about Genesis 2:4 where the Hebrew word for "day," *yôm*, refers to the entire creation week—acknowledges:

> There are many who call even a week one day, because it returns to itself, just as one day does, and one might say seven times revolves back on itself.[31]

One sentence later, he refers to *yôm*'s possible definition as an era or epoch:

> Hence, Scripture appeals at times of an age of the world.[32]

He follows this acknowledgment with the examples of the "day of the Lord" and the "eternal day of reward" in the new creation. Thus, it is not clear how old Ambrose deemed the universe and the earth to be.

Reactions to the Historical Positions

On recent occasions I have met with a jarring reaction to this evidence that the early church fathers were not monolithically aligned in their interpretation of the Genesis creation as a 144-hour time period. That reaction has two prongs: The first is an accusation of syncretism or compromise with Greek philosophy; the second, a dismissal of some early scholars' entire body of work because of "error" in some point of doctrine.

Let's deal with that first prong. Some Greek philosophers posited the notion that the cosmos is eternal, with no beginning or ending. Each of the early Christian leaders quoted above, whether he saw the creation days as long or short, expressed belief that God created the heavens and the earth a finite time ago — a belief clearly and directly at odds with Greek thought. Moreover, far from embracing or accommodating Greek philosophy, Irenaeus and others were scathing in their attacks on it.

And what about the character of these historical figures? Does the "compromiser" label fit men who devoted their lives to refuting false teachers within the church and to challenging secular society's morals, practices, and teachings? Some, like Justin, Irenaeus, and Origen, were either martyred or tortured for their faith in Jesus Christ.

As for the second prong, it grows dull in the light of realistic perspective. Consider the limitations under which they labored — limitations on resources, communications, travel, and so on. They lived and worked during the formative years of the church, most of them before the universal recognition of the New Testament canon. They were attempting to discern and articulate the theological and practical implications of what Christ had taught and what the apostles had written and to integrate all this with what they knew of the Old Testament Scriptures. How unfair to demand of them what even modern scholars with all our resources are incapable of producing — doctrinal perfection!

Fair Conclusions

The time scale of creation, including the length of a creation day, appears to have been something less than a pivotal issue among the early leaders of Christianity. It received little attention compared with such matters as the triune nature of the Godhead, the deity of Christ, or the means, methods, and products of God's creation.

A majority of those who wrote on the subject rejected the concrete interpretation of the Genesis creation days as six consecutive twenty-four-hour periods. However, since so many of the writings of the early Christian leaders have been lost, care must be used in drawing any conclusions based on statistics.

What may be more significant is that these early Christian authors are free of the charge of today's modern scientific bias. They wrote long before astronomical, geological, and paleontological evidences for the antiquity of the universe, of the earth, and of life existed.

Perhaps most significant is that nearly all of the key figures acknowledged that the length of the Genesis creation days presented a challenge to their understanding and interpretation. Those who did not, implied the same in their studious avoidance of any specific comment on the subject.

For the most part the early church leaders expressed their views tentatively. There is no indication that they sharply debated the issue. Instead they seem to have been tolerant of diverse views.

I wish their example had been followed through the centuries. Obviously, it hasn't been. When, where, and how did diversity degenerate to deadly division and discord?

CHAPTER THREE

The Gathering Storm

Throughout the Dark and Middle Ages, church scholars maintained the tolerant attitude of their forefathers toward differing views and interpretations of the creation time scale. However, in the mid-seventeenth century, two British scholars of the newly available *King James Version* produced commentaries bearing the seeds of destructive dissension. In their zeal for exactitude, they inadvertently prepared the soil for what would later grow into a rigid dogmatism, dividing Christian from Christian and faith from fact for centuries to come.

Chronologies of Lightfoot and Ussher

In 1642, just thirty-one years after the completion of the King James translation of the Bible, Cambridge University Vice-Chancellor John Lightfoot completed and published his voluminous (some would say, convoluted) calculation of the exact date for the creation of the universe—September 17, 3928 BC. He drew this conclusion by analyzing the genealogies in Genesis, Exodus, 1 and 2 Kings, and 1 and 2 Chronicles, taking the years cited in the text as precisely 365 days.

Eight years later James Ussher, an Anglican archbishop of Ireland, published his correction of Lightfoot's date for creation, making it October 3, 4004 BC, again with copious commentary and calculations. Ussher's work included his derivation of specific dates for every historical event mentioned in the Bible.[1]

In a final round of academic sparring, Lightfoot made

an adjustment to Ussher's date. He concluded that all creation took place during the week of October 18-24, 4004 BC,
with the creation of Adam occurring on October 23 at 9:00
a.m., forty-fifth meridian time. This extraordinarily precise
conclusion has provoked some mirth among both Bible
scholars and critics.[2]

Ussher and Modern Young-Earth Creationists

Many young-earth creationists react to being labeled as
"Ussherites." Though they agree with Ussher that the
Genesis creation days are six consecutive twenty-four-
hour periods, some deny his assumption that no generations were omitted from the biblical genealogies (for biblical background see chapter 14, pages 139-142).

Young-earth creationists who deny Ussher's assumptions about the genealogies adopt dates for the creation of
the universe anywhere from 10,000 to 50,000 years ago.
From their perspective, the deviation from Ussher's date
is significant. But the difference between their dates and
the range of dates affirmed by science is only about 0.0001
percent. For this reason most scientists see little need to
distinguish between Ussherite and non-Ussherite young-
earthers. From these scientists' perspective, stretching the
6,000 years to 50,000 is inconsequential and does nothing
to enhance credibility.

Perhaps it was the heady atmosphere of England's intellectual ascendency, perhaps it was intellectual intimidation
or ambivalence, but some force worked effectively to
ensconce this 4004 BC date firmly in the minds of millions. It
was taken seriously, with little or no question for more than
a century, though there was much room for question and
critique.

Both Lightfoot and Ussher ignored Hebrew scholarship
and assumed that no generations were omitted from men-

tion in the biblical genealogies. They also assumed, based on the wording of the *King James Version*, that the numbered days of the Genesis creation account could only be six consecutive twenty-four-hour periods.

From the turn of the eighteenth century onward, editions of the King James Bible incorporated Ussher's chronology as margin notes or even as headings in the text. Many readers had difficulty distinguishing the commentator's chronology from the inspired passages. Further, the King James translation quickly became *the* translation for the English-speaking world, and that population became the chief proponent of Protestant Christianity at a time when Christianity was spreading throughout the world.

This intertwining of dates and text—and the lack of serious questioning of the dates for so long—helps us to understand how Ussher's time frame came to be viewed as authoritative by serious Christians nearly everywhere that Protestant Christianity spread.

I say "nearly everywhere" because in one part of the world it met with serious opposition. Though no major objections to Ussher's and Lightfoot's dates for the creation arose in the West during the early and mid-1700s, attempts to spread the Christian gospel in Asia were somewhat stymied because Chinese historical records gave a date for the origin and spread of human civilization earlier than Ussher's date for the origin of the universe.[3] Sadly, this problem drew little if any notice or response among Christians in Europe and the Americas.

Rocks and Fossils Raise Questions

Meanwhile, on the science front, research studies of the earth's crust were getting underway.

In the 1780s, Abraham Werner showed that silt and rocks are deposited in beds or formations in successive layers. In the 1790s, James Hutton studied the differences between sedimentary (water-deposited) and volcanic (lava-deposited) rocks. Then William Smith developed a method for sorting the order of deposition for the sedimentary strata by comparing embedded fossil forms.

By the beginning of the nineteenth century, fossils were recognized as the remains of formerly living things. Meanwhile, fossil hunters unearthed fossilized creatures unlike anything alive today. Georges Cuvier and Jean Lamarck noted that particular fossils relate to particular strata. Subsequently, geologists d'Orbigny, Lyell, Hall, and Hutton concluded from their calculations of geological deposition rates that life must have existed on Earth for at least a quarter of a billion years, with significant, progressive changes over that time.

Most geologists of the day made no claims that life made these changes on its own. Those who stated their hypotheses typically proposed that God had responded to various cosmic and terrestrial catastrophes (e.g., asteroid collisions, volcanos, ice ages, etc.) with separate, successive creations.

Given the entrenchment of Ussher's chronology, it's not difficult to guess what happened when these findings from the new science of geology came to the attention of Christian leaders. A furious attack arose against the geologic time scales. Geologists were accused of slandering the Bible. Yet geologists, at least initially, reaffirmed their belief in a sequence of special, supernatural creations following cosmic or terrestrial catastrophes.[4] They also reminded the world that the Genesis creation account itself portrays a chronological sequence of creations. Most Christians, however, were not appeased. They saw the geologic time scales as a direct attack on the veracity of the Bible.

A Theological Twist

Even before the conflict over sedimentary layers had fully exploded, theology took a sudden turn. It was touched off by the publication of a commentary on Genesis by a French physician who was a pastor's son, Jean Astruc. Astruc argued that Genesis contains two creation narratives, one in the first chapter and another in the second, each written by a different author and each contradicting the other.[5-7]

Astruc began with a detailed, though superficially analyzed, outline of the Genesis 1 creation events. Unfortunately, his chronology was widely accepted even among those who initially resisted his interpretation of the Genesis 2 events and his conclusions about the contradictory order and different authorship of the two passages. Thus Astruc set the stage for a momentous turning point in biblical theology.

Within a few decades, German theologian Johann Eichhorn—seeing that the discoveries of geologists overthrew both the Genesis 1 chronology proposed by Astruc and the time scale firmly fixed since Ussher—proposed a theological "solution." Eichhorn and his German colleagues theorized that at least some, if not much, of the Old Testament is a compilation of late, unreliable documents. From their perspective, the Bible's creation accounts were Hebrew renditions of borrowed myths.

For his championing of this proposition, Eichhorn became known as the father of "higher criticism" theology. For those who embraced it, higher criticism officially severed the cord by which faith had been anchored to fact. *Truth* was thrown open to redefinition.

The initial reaction of both the scientific and the orthodox Christian communities to this new theological perspective was strongly negative. The majority of both groups held to a belief in the inerrancy of the Bible. But the scientists stuck to their geological time scales, while most orthodox Christians clung to Ussher's creation date and Astruc's simplistic chronology.

Gosse's False Age Theory

As scientific evidence for the antiquity of the earth quickly accumulated, scientists who were Christians faced at least one serious problem. One such scientist, Philip Gosse, a British biologist and preacher, acknowledged that paleontological and physical data established an age for the earth far older than a few thousand years.

Gosse the scientist was convinced by the physical evidence that the earth was old, yet Gosse the preacher felt constrained to uphold the date he thought his Christian faith required. How was he to maintain his integrity?

In 1857 Gosse published *Omphalos: An Attempt to Untie the Geological Knot.* To solve his dilemma he introduced the idea that God may have created the earth and life on the earth with the appearance of age. That is, Gosse proposed that God's creation bore false records of the aging process.[8] For example, he believed that God created trees with annual rings for nonexistent years.[9]

Gosse's hypothesis that God had imposed a deceptive appearance on the earth's rocks and on living things struck a sour note with many of his fellow Christians. Though his book did generate strong initial interest, it soon fell from favor, only to await revival by a later generation.

Darwin's Theory Generates Thunderheads

A divinity student turned naturalist, Charles Darwin chose to research the fauna of South America and of certain Pacific islands. Amazed by the diversity of the creatures he found, he pondered how they might have become differentiated to such a degree. While still working to develop a hypothesis, Darwin came across Thomas Malthus's *Essay on Population.*

Thrilled at finding in Malthus's theory a possible explanation for the species' differentiation he had observed, Darwin spent the next twenty years constructing his own theory. In 1859 he presented to the world his *Origins of the Species*, a proposal that all life-forms evolved through natural selection. That is, he theorized that life progressively changed through the preservation of those individual creatures best adapted to survive the competition for existence.

Though acknowledging in the first edition of his book that supernatural assistance from God was necessary to drive biological evolution, Darwin still stirred strong and immediate reaction from the Christian community.

These four major objections to his hypothesis were raised:

- It denied the spontaneous creation of the various species of life.
- It declared life-forms capable of generating new species rather than consistently reproducing after their own kind.
- It denied the special creation of man.
- Its agency of change — natural selection — required vastly more time than the accepted biblical time frame allowed.

Particularly offensive was the descent-of-man concept, the idea that humans descended from lower creatures, specifically from the primates.

Though many scientists strongly objected to Darwin's hypothesis, most, at least within the European scientific community, adopted it with surprising speed, perhaps propelled by the following developments:

- They saw evidence of life-forms changing in response to environmental stress.
- They saw no scientifically supported naturalistic alternative to Darwin's hypothesis.
- They were aware that at least some theological experts, namely the German higher critics, had conceded non-factuality in the biblical texts.
- They were irked by church leaders' emotional diatribes against geologists and the geologic time scales.

The two sides were unavoidably polarized.

CHAPTER FOUR

The Winds of War

The battle that had been brewing since the clash of Light-foot's and Ussher's creation dates with the time scales of contemporary geologists became a thunderous collision of fronts with the publication of Darwin's theory of the origin and development of species. Typically, scientists rushed to one side and Bible-believing Christians to another. The battle's pitch was heightened, I'm sad to say, by personal as much as ideological conflicts.

Monkey-to-Man Debate

Though the Wilberforce–Huxley debate of 1860 is remembered as a confrontation between differing notions of truth, it actually represented a personal grudge match between two biologists. Richard Owen, Britain's foremost biologist of the day, had been humiliated in front of his peers by a younger colleague, Thomas Huxley, at a Royal Society meeting. Soon after that meeting, Huxley publicly praised Darwin's book. Though personally inclined to agree with Darwin, Owen saw an opportunity for revenge. He set up a brilliant orator, the bishop of Oxford, Samuel Wilberforce, to debate Huxley on the subject of Darwin's book.

Wilberforce, with no training in science and only superficial tutoring by Owen, stumbled during the debate into several serious blunders, which Huxley nimbly seized and exposed. His back against the wall, Wilberforce sought a rhetorical victory, asking Huxley if he claimed descent from monkeys on his mother's side. Huxley's brilliant reply will long be remembered:

> I would rather be descended from a poor chattering ape than from a man of great talents who would appeal to prejudice rather than to truth.[1]

These words brought Wilberforce to a shattering defeat. And because scientists viewed Wilberforce as a chief proponent of Christian orthodoxy, the defeat was shattering to public opinion about Christians and Christianity. From that day forward, scientists—not all, but many—associated Christians with prejudice, deception, error, ignorance, emotionalism, and blind opposition to scientific pursuits. It is not uncommon for scientists even to this day to reject Christianity out of hand simply because of reverberations from the Huxley–Wilberforce debate.

Birth of Fundamentalism

The accuracy of Ussher's creation date had become an issue for the Christian faith only when scientific developments of the nineteenth century called that date into question. As the twentieth century dawned, a movement within the church as well as further developments in science brought the age question into the spotlight.

Two American laymen, Milton and Lyman Stewart, between the years 1909 and 1915 financed the publication and broad distribution of twelve small books entitled *The Fundamentals: A Testimony of the Truth*. Without rancor, this set of brief booklets attacked the school of higher criticism theology and reasserted the literal inerrancy of the Bible. The Stewarts emphasized five basic doctrines as absolute essentials for the Christian faith. One was the belief in creation and in humanity's fall from God's grace in Eden.

In 1919, the fundamentalist movement as an organized effort took form with the founding of the World's Christian Fundamentals Association at a conference in Philadelphia.

Subsequent to this meeting, the association took on the task of delineating essentials for qualification as a true Christian, and they went beyond the Stewarts' five fundamentals. In the matter of origins, belief that God created the universe, the earth, and life was no longer enough. The association now deemed evolution, specifically Darwinism, as the great evil of the day. Therefore, Ussher's chronology was adopted as a necessary doctrine, the only defense they recognized for stemming the rising tide of godless science.

In just ten years, the movement launched by Milton and Lyman Stewart had evolved from a careful, dispassionate defense of Christian orthodoxy to a combative, emotionally charged crusade. One newspaper reporter in 1920 characterized the group as those who fought "battle royal for the Fundamentals."[2]

The Monkey Trial

Fundamentalist attacks on Darwinism and counterattacks by scientists and others escalated after the 1925 Scopes trial. William Jennings Bryan, three-time presidential candidate and noted fundamentalist, handled the prosecution of a biology teacher who intentionally defied Tennessee's law against teaching evolution in the public schools. Unwittingly Bryan stepped into a carefully laid trap. Scopes, the teacher, was found guilty, as expected, but the prosecutor's victory in this trial has long been overshadowed by what happened in the witness chair.

Bryan himself took the stand as an expert witness on the fundamentals of the Christian faith. Under the crafty cross-examination of defense attorney Clarence Darrow, Bryan was forced to admit that the six, consecutive, twenty-four-hour periods he affirmed as *the* biblical truth of creation must be incorrect. Darrow forced Bryan into conceding that the Genesis creation days must be longer time periods.[3] Darrow then simply let the judge, the courtroom spectators, and the world outside conclude that Christians had no real case against Darwinism.

Shocked by Bryan's disgrace, many fundamentalists became convinced that bolting the door on the geologic time scale was their only hope for upholding the Bible as true. They decided to cement belief in a universe only thousands of years old into their doctrinal position on creation. In effect, the five fundamentals of the faith became six.

Molecules to Man

Following World War II, Darwinist hypotheses were expanded into the molecules-to-man concept. With the philosophy of naturalism now permeating the scientific community, who would question the notion that biological evolution by strictly natural means extended not just to primitive cells but all the way back to inorganic chemicals? Origin-of-life researchers admitted they were a long way from synthesizing life in the laboratory and from observing the production of *any* organic molecules from inorganic material either on the earth or in outer space. But they nonetheless so influenced other scientists and educators that high school biology texts began teaching molecules-to-man as a solidly established, fact-based theory.[4]

Nothing could have inflamed Bible-believing Christians more than the molecules-to-man concept. It was recognized as a thinly veiled attempt to eliminate God from having *anything* to do with life or with humans. At the same time, fundamentalists were acutely aware that if they were to gain any clout with the educational and political establishments in thwarting the evolutionists' claims, they would have to build their case on scientific credibility.

Enter Scientific Creationism

In 1961 Henry Morris, a civil engineering professor, and John Whitcomb, a theology professor, published a book entitled *The Genesis Flood*.[5] This lengthy volume dealt with much more than the Flood. It was a treatise on creation according to the young-universe time scale of thousands of years. It read like a scientific text and included all the trappings of one. To fundamentalists, *The Genesis Flood* gave the intellectual and scientific respectability they had been seeking. They could now combat science with science, or so it seemed.

Stimulated by the publication of *The Genesis Flood*, ten fundamentalist scientists banded together in 1963 to form the Creation Research Society (CRS). Within ten years the CRS boasted 450 members with graduate degrees in science. This rapidly growing group of scientifically trained creationists brought about a spectacular promulgation of young-universe teaching. By 1970 the CRS began to splinter because of differences in personalities and objectives, but this splintering served only to multiply the CRS's impact.

The Creation-Science Research Center (CSRC) was formed in 1970 to specialize in gaining legal recognition for the teaching of scientific creationism (i.e., young-universe creationism) in schools. By that year, the teaching of evolution had become legal, as well as predominant, in all states. The Institute for Creation Research (ICR), formed in 1972, focused on research, education, and public lectures and debates. Since then, several dozen young-universe creationist organizations have proliferated across the United States.

By 1980 nearly every American evangelical church and school had been strongly influenced by the young-universe creationist organizations and teachings. In fact, their influence had spread around the world. Societies along the lines of the CRS and the ICR formed in more than two dozen nations. So pervasive has been the influence of such groups that their views on creation are thought to represent the doctrine of the entire community of Bible-believing Christians. The word *creationist* implies the young-universe position, though many orthodox Christians who believe in creation (and deny Darwinism) hold different views regarding the timing of creation.

Science Establishment Strikes Back

The science establishment tended to treat young-universe creationists as they would flat-earth proponents. For a while most scientists simply presumed that the evidences against the young-universe, young-earth hypotheses were so obvious and overwhelming that no rebuttal was necessary. In fact, rebutting this premise was discouraged because it would yield undue attention and the tiniest hint of academic merit to the young-earth view. Not until they saw the threat of laws forcing the teaching of scientific creationism did the science establishment lash out.

America's most influential scientific body, the American Association for the Advancement of Science (AAAS), began publishing articles in its technical journal, Science, pointing out the dangers and errors of scientific creationism.[6-11] Later, the AAAS published a special insert section in its popular-level magazine, Science 81, challenging creationism as non-science.[12-14] Copies of this insert were distributed to the 100,000 members of the National Science Teachers Association in 1981.[15]

In 1983 the National Center for Science Education (NCSE) was founded to support and coordinate "committees of correspondence." At least one such committee exists in every state of the U. S. and in five Canadian provinces. The declared purpose of NCSE and these committees is to "keep scientific creationism from being taught as legitimate science."[16]

Deepening Polarization

Neither creationists nor evolutionists have seriously sought resolution to this controversy. Rather both have heightened animosity by perceiving and portraying their opponents as irrational, evil extremists.

Edward Blick accuses evolutionists of "deliberately bluffing," of making "patently false" statements, of violating rules of logic through "circular reasoning, faulty premises, faulty analogies, and wishful thinking," and of making a farce of scientific laws.[17] Henry Morris blames evolutionary uniformitarianism for spawning "the vast complex of godless movements."[18]

Evolutionist Thomas Jukes accuses the young-earth creationists of using "terrorist tactics."[19] "The irresponsible mis-
representation of science that is habitually demonstrated by
creationists" elicits "justifiable anger," according to geologist
Richard Bambach.[20]

With both sides accusing the other of distortion, deceit,
and bad science, little hope of reconciliation has been seen or
expressed. Each side enrolls large numbers of followers. A
1982 Gallup poll reported that 44 percent of Americans held
to a 10,000-year-old creation date while 47 percent held to
some form of Darwinian evolution. The degree of tension
between these two groups is demonstrated by the 74 percent
of those surveyed who wanted to see only their own view
taught in the public schools.[21]

Resurgence of "Appearance of Age"

Attempting a creative and convenient end run around the
science establishment, young-universe creationists have
revived and slightly revised Gosse's "appearance of age"
concept. Gary North, an influential "reconstructionist" theologian (see page 39 for more on reconstructionism) makes
this statement:

> The Bible's account of the chronology of creation points
> to an illusion. . . . The seeming age of the stars is an illu-
> sion. . . . Either the constancy of the speed of light is an
> illusion, or the size of the universe is an illusion, or else
> the physical events that we hypothesize to explain the
> visible changes in light or radiation are false inferences.[22]

The Institute for Creation Research (ICR), now the most
prominent and vocal advocate of a few-thousands-of-years-
old universe and earth, relies to some degree on this theory
of apparent versus real age.

Henry Morris, ICR's president, implies that no tool of
science can ever yield real information on the age of the
earth:

The compelling Biblical . . . direct testimony from the Creator is the *only* way to *know* the age of the earth.[23] (italics in original)

Reconstructionism and Presuppositionalism

Reconstructionism, as taught by Gary North and others, is a doctrinal system combining Puritan beliefs about law, politics, and biblical end-times events with Cornelius Van Til's theological theory called presuppositionalism. Presuppositionalism, as taught by Van Til and his associates, says that all human reasoning and interpretation of scientific evidence must be subordinated to a "biblical" interpretation of reality.

Presuppositionalism, as expounded by many modern creationists, has evolved to the claim that *any* scientific interpretation of the record of nature can be discounted in the light of interpretations of the words of the Bible. For a thorough definition and helpful analysis see *Dominion Debate: Kingdom Theology and Christian Reconstruction in Biblical Perspective* by Robert M. Bowman, Jr. (Baker , 1991).

Marvin Lubenow, an ICR associate, concurs:

> There is no general Bible-science conflict if one recognizes the domain of science to be primarily in the present and involving the investigation of *present-day* phenomena.[24] (italics in original)

John Whitcomb, another ICR associate, prefers the term "superficial appearance of history or age"[25]:

> There could be no *genuine* creation of any kind without an initial appearance of age inherent in it. . . . *If God exists!* — then there is no reason why He could not, in full conformity with His character of truth, create a whole universe full-grown.[26] (italics in original)

Appearance of Age and Illusions

Gary North is right. A creation date for the universe of only thousands of years implies that in some respect the universe must be an illusion. Since astronomers believe they have sound reasons for concluding that the universe is real (see chapter 9), they are naturally reluctant to adopt young-universe creationism. However, this divorce from physical reality extends beyond the denial of distant stars and galaxies.

Taken to its logical conclusion, the appearance-of-age hypothesis would imply that we cannot establish the actuality of our own or others' past existence. We could have been created just a few hours ago with the Creator implanting scars, memory, progeny, photographs, material possessions, liver spots, and hardening of the arteries to make us appear and feel older than we really are. Also, if God built into the universe natural testimony of events which never took place, how can we claim the Bible is free of written testimony of events which never took place?

An independent young-universe creationist, Lambert Dolphin, boldly claims that time did not begin until Adam's rebellion in the Garden of Eden,[27] and then states:

> The fact that pre-history occurred before t = 0 gives our universe an appearance of great age.[28]

Another independent, Dennis Petersen, in response to the question, "What about all those stars that are millions of light years away?" responds, "If your God could create sources of star light, do you think He might be able to create the light beams to instantly appear on the Earth?"[29]

The appearance of age argument provides a consoling response to the overwhelming scientific evidence for a billions-of-years-old universe and earth. If the age of things in the realm of nature is indeed illusory, then no amount of scientific evidence means anything against young-earth interpretations of the words of the Bible. These interpretations, thus, remain safe and secure from outside influences. Science—at least the science research of secular institutions—ceases to matter.

Single-Revelation Theology

Advocates of the appearance-of-age theory typically hold what is called a single revelation view—belief that the Bible is the only authoritative source of truth. In other words, we "must grope in darkness apart from God's special revelation in Scripture."[30] No departure from literal interpretations of the Bible can be tolerated ("literal" is taken to mean a concrete and nonfigurative reading of the text).

Morris takes for granted that the deeply rooted scientific "assumption" of an old universe provides the *only* basis for taking the Genesis creation days as anything other than twenty-four-hour days:

> The road of compromise [on the issue of age, for example], however attractive it seems, is a one-way street, ending in a precipice and then the awful void of "rational religion," or atheism. Our advice is to stay on the straight road of the pure Word of God.[31]

North agrees:

> For Christians to tamper with the plain meaning of the Bible in order to make it conform to the latest findings of this or that school of evolutionary thought is nothing short of disastrous.[32]

Morris, North, and others ignore or reject the biblical scholarship and sincerity of faith of those who show that the Hebrew texts allow ample room for, or—as I believe—strongly suggest, a different interpretation of the words for the creation days.

The Battle Blocks the Path

Because of the outspokenness of young-universe creationists, most people now assume that the Bible directly declares
God created everything in 144 hours about six to ten thousand years ago. And because of the scientific implausibility
of such a position, many people reject the Bible without seriously investigating its message or even reading for themselves what it says.

Most secularists with whom I have discussed this issue
perceive that becoming a Christian requires them to reject all
authority but the words of the Bible. Few have been presented with the possibility of God's dual revelation of truth.
Dual revelation means that since God is responsible for both
the biblical revelation and the natural world, the words of
the Bible are true and at the same time consistent with the
facts of nature. His character and attributes are expressed
through both channels, and neither negates nor contradicts
the other. This viewpoint represents an obvious but rarely
articulated option.

All too often, people are left with the hard choice
between believing what they think are the words of the Bible
(actually, a particular interpretation) and rejecting the facts
of nature *or* believing the facts of nature and rejecting the
words of the Bible. Christians have tragically set up a false
dilemma that creates barriers to serious consideration of the
really crucial spiritual issues.

Wounds Within the Ranks

With rising hostilities on both sides of the creation-evolution
controversy, some Christians seem to be growing even more
dogged in their defense of a recent creation. Many churches
and Bible colleges now include belief in a young universe
and a young earth in their statement of faith. In some cases,
applicants who disagree are denied admission.

In 1992 the Institute for Creation Research published an
article in its *Back to Genesis* magazine about the importance
of belief in a young earth for determining a person's role in

the church and in ministry. The article's author, John Morris, ends with this statement:

> I still am uncertain about young-earth creationism being a requirement for church membership; perhaps it would be proper to give new members time to grow and mature under good teaching. But I do know one thing: [young-earth] Creationism *should* be made a requirement for Christian leadership! No church should sanction a pastor, Sunday school teacher, deacon, elder, or Bible-study leader who knowledgeably and purposefully errs on this crucial doctrine.[33] (italics in original)

Even where adherence to young-earth creationism is not declared in writing, it may be potently expressed. A young astronomy research assistant and his wife seeking Christian fellowship were asked to leave one church after another, not because of anything they did or said, but simply because in response to probing they acknowledged their belief that the universe is some billions of years old. A world-renowned astronomer met with similar difficulty. After coming to personal faith in Jesus Christ, he sought a church home where he would not have to hide his identity and beliefs. He checked out more than fifty evangelical churches before finding one that upheld the Bible as the error-free Word of God and also tolerated belief in an old universe and earth.

Addressing the Damage

Is it any wonder that individuals trained in the sciences, especially those with little or no Christian background, find it difficult to make their way into churches? How painful to be a disciple of Christ or a sincere seeker and yet be regarded as an enemy of the faith!

How difficult, too, for the devout fundamentalist, trained as he is to stand firm against compromise and worldly thinking, to embrace as a brother or sister anyone who believes in a billions-of-years-old universe or earth! According to what he has been taught, such people must be evil, for they can only be evolutionists.

With these dynamics at work, open, friendly dialogue has become virtually impossible. Instead heated debates, confrontations, public attacks, and watchdog committees rule the day.

Now is the time to call for a cease-fire. Now is the time to bend every effort—short of compromising either the words of the Bible or the facts of nature—toward a peaceful resolution. Let's go back to where the battle began. Let's reconsider the assumptions that propelled it. Let's acknowledge our emotional attachment to our views and with a sense of humility, and perhaps some humor, plunge ahead with our reconsiderations, trusting God's Spirit to guide us. What better place to begin than with Scripture itself? What does the Bible say, and what does it not say, about the time frame of God's creative work?

CHAPTER FIVE

Biblical Basis for Long Creation Days

Genesis 1 states that within six "days" God miraculously transformed a "formless and void" earth into a suitable habitat for humanity and then created human beings from dust. The meaning of the word *day*, of course, is the focal point of the creation time-scale controversy. Does it, or does it not, represent a contradiction between Scripture and science?

The answer to that question depends on whether the time period indicated must be a twenty-four-hour day or whether it can refer to something like millions of years. Most Bible scholars would agree that a correct and literal interpretation takes into account definitions, context, grammar, and relevant passages from other parts of Scripture.

While young-earth creationists assert the "plain meaning" of the text rules out all but twenty-four-hour creation days, a careful look at various textual elements points to a different conclusion. Old-earth creationists find many scriptural reasons, apart from science, for interpreting the creation days as long time periods. Here are key considerations:

1. *The length of God's days.* The same author of Genesis (Moses) wrote in Psalm 90:4, "For a thousand years in your sight are like a day that has just gone by, or like a watch [four hours] in the night." Moses seems to state that just as God's ways are not our ways (Isaiah 55:9), God's days are not our days.

2. *The Hebrew words* yôm, 'ereb, *and* boqer. The Hebrew word *yôm*, translated *day*, may be used (and is) in biblical Hebrew, as it is in modern English, to indicate any of three time periods: (a) sunrise to sunset, (b) sunset to sunset, (c) a segment of time without any reference to solar days (anywhere from weeks to a year to several years to an age or epoch). This does not mean, however, that *yôm* can be interpreted as referring to an indefinite time or infinite time.

William Wilson, in his *Old Testament Word Studies*, explains that *yôm* is "frequently put for time in general, or for a long time, a whole period under consideration. . . . Day [*yôm*] is also put for a particular season or time when any extraordinary event happens."[1]

Even in English—which includes many more words than Hebrew for describing time periods—such expressions as "my grandfather's day" or "the day of the dinosaurs" are common. Biblical examples would be Genesis 4:3 (*yôm* = process of time); Genesis 30:14 (*yôm* = wheat harvest time); Joshua 24:7 (*yôm* = a long season); Proverbs 25:13 (*yôm* = harvest time); Isaiah 4:2 (*yôm* = a future era); Zechariah 14:8 (*yôm* = summer + winter); and many references to the day of the Lord (*yôm* = forty-two months or more, depending on one's interpretation of certain end-time prophecies).

The Hebrew word *'ereb*, translated *evening*, also means "sunset," "night," or "ending of the day."[2,3] And the word *boqer*, translated *morning*, also means "sunrise," "coming of light," "beginning of day," "break of day," or "dawning," with possible metaphoric usage.[4,5]

In other words, evening and morning refer to the beginning and ending components of "day," however it is used. For example, "in my grandfather's day" refers to my grandfather's lifetime. So the morning and evening of his day would be his youth and old age.

Young-earth creationists have argued for twenty-four-hour days on the basis that *yôm* when attached to an ordinal (second, third, fourth, etc.) always refers to a twenty-four-hour period. This argument can be challenged on several counts. For one, it is true only for passages describing days of human activity rather than days of divine activity. For another, nowhere else does the Bible have the occasion to enumerate sequential epochs. More important, the rules of Hebrew grammar do not require that *yôm* must refer to twenty-four hours, even when attached to an ordinal.

Hosea 6:2 prophesies that "after two days he [God] will revive us [Israel]; on the third day he will restore us." For centuries Bible commentators have noted that the "days" in this passage (where the ordinal is used) refer to a year, years, a thousand years, or maybe more.[6-8]

Young-earthers also hold the view that the Hebrew word *'olam* (as opposed to *yôm*) would have been used to indicate a long time period. However, Hebrew lexicons show that only in post-biblical writings did *'olam* only refer to a long age or epoch. In biblical times it meant "forever," "perpetual," "lasting," "always," "of olden times," or "the remote past, future, or both." But the range of its usage did not include a set period of time.[9-10]

3. *The function of a chronology.* A study of other chronologies in the Bible reveals a common characteristic: They record sequences that are both significant and discernible to the reader. The timing and order are important because they show the careful unfolding of God's plans and affirm His control. The discernibility provides a tool for validating the message of God's spokesmen. Examples from my own theological perspective include: Jeremiah 31:38-40 (a prediction, now fulfilled, of the location and construction sequence of Jerusalem's nine suburbs during the second rebirth of Israel as a nation); Daniel 9:24-27 (a timetable for the rebuilding of Jerusalem, the Messiah's coming and death, the destruction of Jerusalem, years of desolation, and final restoration); and Daniel 11:2-35 (a prediction, since fulfilled, of the chronology of victories, defeats, and intrigues of various kings and kingdoms of the Greek and Roman eras). The supernatural accuracy of such chronologies not only proves their inspiration but also gives assurance for today and hope for tomorrow.

Recorded events not intended to be time discernible to the reader are presented without the use of sequence markers. For example, in Acts 6 Luke does not indicate the order in which the first seven deacons of the church were chosen. He lists the names in random order because there was no special significance to the order of their selection.

For the creation days, long time periods during which increasingly complex life-forms were created, indeed, are verifiable and essential to validate the supernatural accuracy of the writer's statements. But if all creation were completed in six twenty-four-hour days, the most sophisticated measuring techniques available, or even foreseeably available, would be totally incapable of discerning the sequence of events. Thus a major use of the chronology would be thwarted.

4. *The unusual syntax of the sentences enumerating specific creation days.* Looking at the word-for-word translation of the Hebrew text, one finds this phraseology: "and was evening and was morning day X." *The New International Version* phrases the time markers this way: "And there was evening, and there was morning—the Xth day." The word arrangement is clearly a departure from simple and ordinary expression. It creates an ambiguity. If "day X" were intended as the noun complement for the one evening and morning together, the linking verb should appear just once, in plural form (as the *King James Version* renders it): "And the evening and the morning were the Xth day." We would expect the literal Hebrew to say, "and were evening and morning day X." But it does not. This syntactic ambiguity does not constitute a proof. However, it does suggest that "day" here is to be taken in some unusual manner.

5. *The uniqueness of the seventh day.* Of the first six creation days Moses wrote: "There was evening, and there was morning—the Xth day." This wording indicates that each of the first six creation days had a beginning and an ending. However, no such wording is attached to the seventh creation day, neither in Genesis 1–2 nor anywhere else in the Bible. Given the parallel structure marking the creation days,

this distinct change in form for the seventh day strongly suggests that this day has (or had) not yet ended.

Further information about the seventh day is given in Psalm 95 and Hebrews 4. In these passages we learn that God's day of rest continues. The writer of Hebrews stated,

> For somewhere he [God] has spoken about the seventh day in these words: "And on the seventh day God rested from all his work." . . . It still remains that some will enter that rest. . . . There remains, then, a Sabbath-rest for the people of God; for anyone who enters God's rest also rests from his own work, just as God did from his. Let us, therefore, make every effort to enter that rest. (4:4-11)

According to this passage, the seventh day of the creation week carries on through the centuries, from Adam and Eve, through Israel's development as a nation, through the time of Christ's earthly ministry, through the early days of the church, and on into future years. King David in Psalm 95:7-11 also refers to God's seventh day of rest as ongoing.

From these passages we gather that the seventh day of Genesis 1 and 2 represents a minimum of several thousand years and a maximum that is open ended (but finite). It seems reasonable to conclude then, given the parallelism of the Genesis creation account, that the first six days may also have been long time periods.

Supporting evidence for the seventh day as an ongoing period of rest from creating comes from John 5:16-18. Here, Jesus defended His healing on the Sabbath by saying that God, His Father, "is always at his work to this very day, and I, too, am working." Jesus' appeal is that He is honoring the Sabbath the same way His Father is. That is, His Father works "to this very day" even though this very day is part of His Sabbath rest period. God—both the Son and Father—honors His Sabbath by ceasing from the work of creating. The Sabbath does not preclude healing people any more than it precludes a man from changing his baby's diaper on his day off from work.

The fossil record provides further confirmation of an ongoing seventh day, a day of cessation from creative activity. According to the fossils, more and more species of life came into existence through the millennia before modern man. The number of species going extinct nearly balanced the number of introductions, but introductions remained at least slightly more numerous. Then came human beings.

In the years of human history, the extinction rate for species of life has remained high while the introduction rate measures a virtual zero. Estimates of the current extinction rate vary widely, from a low of one species per day to a high of five species per hour.[11,12] Though humanity's influence on that rate is significant,[13] even without it, at least one species per year goes extinct.[14,15]

As biologists Paul and Anne Ehrlich report, "The production of a new animal species in nature has yet to be documented." Furthermore, "In the vast majority of cases, the rate of change is so slow that it has not even been possible to detect an increase in the amount of differentiation."[16] Obviously a tremendous imbalance between extinctions and speciation now exists.

The creation days of Genesis, if long, provide an explanation. For six days (the fossil record eras) God created new life-forms. After the creation of Adam and Eve, however, God ceased from His work of creating new life-forms (the seventh day), and His rest, or "cessation," continues to this day. (He is still at work in other, providential ways.)

6. *The events of the sixth day.* Genesis 1 tells us that the land mammals and *both* Adam and Eve were created on the sixth day. Genesis 2 provides further amplification, listing events between Adam's creation and Eve's. First, God planted a garden in Eden, making "all kinds of trees to grow out of the ground." Then Adam, after receiving instructions from God, worked and cared for the Garden of Eden. After that, he carried out his assignment from God to name all the

animals (the *nephesh* creatures—i.e., all the birds and mammals). In the process Adam discovered that none of these creatures was a suitable helper and companion for him.

Apparently Adam had sufficient interaction with the plants and animals of the garden to realize that something was missing from his life. Next, God put Adam into a deep sleep, performed an operation and, after Adam awoke, introduced him to the newly created Eve.

Adam's exclamation on seeing Eve is recorded in Genesis 2:23 as *happa'am*. This expression is usually translated as "now at length" (see also Genesis 29:34-35, 30:20, 46:30; Judges 15:3), roughly equivalent to our English expression "at last."

Still later on the sixth day Adam and Eve received instructions from God concerning their responsibilities in managing the plants, animals, and resources of the earth, a lengthy communication, one can imagine. Altogether, many weeks', months', or even years' worth of activities took place in this latter portion of the sixth day.

Some twenty-four-hour proponents argue that Adam's intelligence was so much higher before he sinned that he could do all these tasks at superhuman speed. This argument fails to account for Adam's response to Eve and, just as important, for the following five matters:

a. There is no biblical basis for suggesting Adam functioned at superhuman speeds before he sinned.
b. The Bible never claims that intellect (as opposed to wisdom) is correlated with the degree of sin in one's life. Intellect is not a reliable measure of freedom from sin.
c. Greater intellect would not significantly impact Adam's sixth-day tasks and experiences.
d. Adam in his perfect state would be all the more meticulous in performing his God-assigned tasks.
e. Jesus, though He was perfect in every way, did not perform His carpentry work and other everyday activities at a much faster than normal rate.

7. *The wording of Genesis 2:4.* This verse, a summary statement for the creation account, in the literal Hebrew reads, "These are the generations of the heavens and the earth when they were created in the day of their making." Here the word *day* refers to all six creation days (and the creation of the universe that took place prior to the first creative day). Obviously, then, this is a period longer than twenty-four hours. Hebrew lexicons verify that the word for generation (*toledah*) refers to the time between a person's birth and parenthood or to an arbitrarily longer time span.[17] In Genesis 2:4 the plural form, *generations*, is used, indicating that multiple generations have passed.

8. *Biblical figures of speech for the earth's age.* In describing the eternity of God's existence, several Bible writers often compare it to the longevity of the mountains or the "foundations of the earth." The figures of speech used in Psalm 90:2-6, Proverbs 8:22-31, Ecclesiastes 1:3-11, and Micah 6:2 all depict the immeasurable antiquity of God's presence and plans. The brief span of a 3000-year terrestrial history (in the context of the wisdom literature) seems an inadequate metaphor for God's eternality. The fact that the Bible does consider the antiquity of the founding of the earth a suitable metaphor for God's eternality suggests the biblical view of a very ancient earth.

9. *Explicit statements of earth's antiquity.* Habakkuk 3:6 directly declares that the mountains are "ancient" and the hills are "age-old." In 2 Peter 3:5, the heavens (the stars and the universe) are said to have existed "long ago."

Conclusion

Though not an exhaustive treatment of the subject, these nine considerations come from Bible passages directly addressing the length of the creation days. Many more Bible passages implicitly or indirectly refer to the timing of creation. Such passages must be studied and understood in the context of larger theological issues. Let's move on to a look at these.

CHAPTER SIX

Theological Basis for Long Creation Days

As early church leaders admitted, many Bible passages that address or allude to the ages of the universe and the earth are difficult to interpret. Such passages require careful analysis of both context and relevant theological issues. Failure to be cautious and complete in such analysis can lead to inaccurate conclusions. Ironically, some of the passages cited to support a young-universe view may in fact be used to support an old-universe interpretation. What follows is a list of ten theological considerations that bear significantly on the interpretation of biblical references to creation and time:

1. *God is truthful and desires to reveal truth, both in the creation and in the written Word. He does not trick or deceive.* Jesus, the visible expression of the invisible God, said to His disciples, "I am the truth." In this statement He verbally expressed one of His divine attributes. Many familiar Bible verses explicitly declare that God is truthful and that He does not lie, either in word or in deed. Neither does He hide the truth from those who seek to find it. Even the desire to search for truth comes from Him. (See, for example, Psalm 119:160; Isaiah 45:19; John 8:31-32, 10:35; Titus 1:2; Hebrews 6:18, 11:6; 1 John 5:6.)

Our view of creation must take God's character into account. Whatever objects of His creation we subject to scientific analysis will reveal their true age—provided the analysis is theoretically valid, correctly applied, and accurately interpreted. For created things to show a deceptive appearance of age would seem a direct violation of God's own stated character and purpose.

While the Bible teaches that God created Adam and Eve with adult-sized bodies and adult capabilities, it does not state that God put into them several years of deterioration. As anyone who has observed children will realize, size and capability are not by themselves reliable indicators of age.

We must consider, too, that Adam and Eve were made, not born. We would not infer any age from the size and capability of Adam's and Eve's bodies given our awareness, from God's own report, that Adam and Eve were created as exceptions to the subsequent natural rule.

Reliable age indicators for human beings do exist, however. Liver spots on the skin, scar tissue, muscle and skin tone, visual acuity, blood and bone chemistry, and memories of past events provide fairly accurate measures of human age. I'm willing to speculate that tests of these age indicators in Adam and Eve would have revealed their true age. (The context of Genesis 3:22-24 seems to imply that Adam and Eve had not yet partaken of the tree of life. Of course, that at least to some extent would have obviated the aging process.)

Another biblical example sometimes quoted as evidence for appearance of age is Jesus' first public miracle: turning water into wine. The text (John 2:7-10) states, however, that the wine Jesus miraculously made had superb flavor, flavor which in this case did not necessarily come from an acceleration of the aging process. Modern methods exist for measuring the true age of a wine, but taste is not one of them.

Neither Adam and Eve nor the water Jesus turned into wine are available for accurate age testing. Adam and Eve died. The wine was consumed. Therefore, neither should be brought forward as evidence supporting appearance of age.

But the universe and the earth *are* available. The abundant and consistent evidence from astronomy, physics, geology, and paleontology must be taken seriously.

2. The Bible affirms that the creation reveals God's existence, His handiwork, His power, and His divine nature. Romans 1:20 and Colossians 1:23, among other passages, make clear that the physical universe we see and experience sufficiently proves God's existence and identity as Creator of all things. The creation itself also shows humanity His love, power, wisdom, provision, and protection—to name just a few of His qualities—so that all "men are without excuse."

It seems reasonable to conclude, then, that honest investigation of nature leads to discovery of truths, including truths about God and about His otherwise invisible qualities. We are "without excuse" because the physical universe speaks truly. How could we be held accountable by God for our response to a distorted message?

This revelation of God via the universe in no way detracts from the importance of His written revelation, nor does it imply that God never intervenes in the realm of nature by performing miracles. For example, God certainly had the power to alter the laws of physics at the instant that Adam sinned against God. But we can be confident that He did not since the astronomical record shows no evidence of such an alteration. (See pages 96-100 for an explanation of why astronomy provides an inviolable testimony of past natural history.) What the revelation of God through creation implies is that God does not remove, hide, or distort the physical evidence of the miracles He performs.

3. The Bible affirms that the Word of God includes not only the words of the Bible but also His words written on the heavens and the earth. Many young-universe creationists limit the Word of God to the words of the Bible. Since the Bible declares that only God and His Word *are* truth, these creationists consider information from any source outside the Bible as inferior and suspect. To them, extrabiblical data holds little value for clarifying what the Bible teaches on any issue or for prompting correction of faulty interpretation.

Yet the Bible more than once says God speaks through the creation. According to Psalm 19:1-4:

The heavens declare the glory of God; the skies proclaim the work of his hands. Day after day they pour
forth speech; night after night they display knowledge.
There is no speech or language where their voice is not
heard. Their voice goes out into all the earth, their
words to the ends of the world.

Psalm 85:11 reads, "Truth springs from the earth; and righteousness looks down from heaven" (NASB). The Hebrew
word for truth, *emet*, basically means "certainty and depend-
ability."[1] Addressing his three friends, Job challenges them:

Ask the animals, and they will teach you, or the birds of
the air, and they will tell you; or speak to the earth, and
it will teach you, or let the fish of the sea inform you.
(Job 12:7-8)

It would follow from these and other verses that, in
addition to the words of the Bible being "God-breathed, . . .
useful for teaching, rebuking, correcting, and training in
righteousness" (2 Timothy 3:16), so also are the words of
God spoken through the work of His hands.

In other words, the Bible teaches a dual, reliably consistent revelation. God has revealed Himself through the words
of the Bible and the facts of nature. According to Psalm
19:1-4, the "words" of God proclaimed through the stars and
galaxies are constantly being read by all peoples unto the
ends of the earth. In Romans 1:19-20, the Bible declares that
everyone is "without excuse" as he or she faces God's eternal judgment (including people who have never read the
Bible or heard the gospel from believers), since what may be
known about God has been made plain to *all* through what
has been created. Colossians 1:23 states that salvation "has
been proclaimed to every creature under heaven."

So, God's revelation is not limited exclusively to the
Bible's words. The facts of nature may be likened to a sixty-
seventh book of the Bible. Just as we rightfully expect inter-

pretations of Isaiah to be consistent with those of Mark, so too we can expect interpretations of the facts of nature to be consistent with the message of Genesis and the rest of the canon.

The "Voice" of Nature

Many Bible passages state that God reveals Himself faithfully through the "voice" of nature as well as through the inspired words of Scripture. Here is a partial list of such verses:

Job 10:8-14	Psalm 104
Job 12:7	Psalm 139
Job 34:14-15	Proverbs 8:22-31
Job 35:10-12	Ecclesiastes 3:11
Job 37:5-7	Habakkuk 3:3
Job 38-41	Acts 14:17
Psalm 8	Acts 17:23-31
Psalm 19:1-6	Romans 1:18-25
Psalm 50:6	Romans 2:14-15
Psalm 85:11	Romans 10:16-18
Psalm 97:6	Colossians 1:23
Psalm 98:2-3	

Some readers might fear I am implying that God's revelation through nature is somehow on an equal footing with His revelation through the words of the Bible. Let me simply state that truth, by definition, is information that is perfectly free of contradiction and error. Just as it is absurd to speak of some entity as more perfect than another, so also one revelation of God's truth cannot be held as inferior or superior to another. It could be different, just like the content of Ezra is distinct from that of Romans, but it cannot be better or worse. Thus when science appears to conflict with theology, we have no reason to reject either the facts of nature or the Bible's words. Rather, we have reason to reexamine our interpretations of those facts and words because sound science and sound biblical exegesis will always be in harmony.

This dual and perfectly harmonious revelation reflects God's character and purpose. God is truth, speaks truth, guides us into truth, and does not lie.[2] From both the Bible and the record of nature we can establish that God is totally responsible for the existence of the universe.[3-5] And, according to both the Bible and the records of nature and history, God is responsible for the words of the Bible.[6-8] Therefore, no contradiction between the facts of nature and the facts of the Bible is possible. Any apparent contradiction must stem from human misunderstanding.

4. The Bible writers describe the vastness of the universe. In Genesis 22:17, Jeremiah 33:22, and Hebrews 11:12, the number of God's children is compared with the number of stars in the sky and the number of grains of sand on the seashore — a "countless" number, i.e., beyond a few billion.

The Hebrew (and Greek) numbering systems included numbers up to the billions. "Countless" would indicate a number at least one order of magnitude greater than billions: tens of billions. These biblical statements of vastness are important as translated into a statement about age. Given tens of billions (100 billion) of stars as a minimum, and noting that the stars in our galaxy are separated from each other by average distances of about ten light years, we can use the standard equation for the volume of a sphere to calculate that the diameter of the universe must be no less than 56,000 light years. Since no material in our universe moves more rapidly than the velocity of light,[9] and since the velocity of light must remain constant for life to exist (see pages 97-99), we can conclude that the biblically stated *minimum* age for the universe is 56,000 years.

Other "vastness" data show that the universe is much greater yet, and we see no evidence violating that minimum. The galaxy of which our sun is a member star contains one-hundred billion stars. Its shape, however, resembles a flattened disk rather than a sphere. That disk has a measured diameter of 120,000 light years. Those light years translate into a minimum age for the cosmos of 120,000 years.

According to recent findings, the number of stars in the universe totals approximately 10^{23} (a number that also approximates the sum of the grains of sand on the seashores, as the Bible metaphorically suggests). Again, using size to indicate age, 10^{23} stars separated from one another by about ten light years (a gross underestimate for the whole universe) would indicate a minimum diameter of 580 million light years, thus a minimum age of 580 million years.

Note: God certainly has the power to construct the universe at a more rapid rate than the velocity of light, but the physical evidence indicates that He did not do so (astronomers' observations of the past, see pages 97-100). Let me repeat an earlier point: A consistent pattern in God's revelations is that when He does perform miracles, He does not purposefully remove or intentionally hide the evidence of those miracles from us.

5. The Sabbath day for man and Sabbath year for the land are analogous to God's work week. God's fourth commandment says that the seventh day of each week is to be honored as holy, "For in six days the LORD made the heavens and the earth . . . but he rested on the seventh day" (Exodus 20:10-11). This passage is often cited as proof positive for the twenty-four-hour-day interpretation. Evangelical Hebrew scholar Gleason Archer disagrees: "By no means does this demonstrate that 24-hour intervals were involved in the first six 'days,' any more than the eight-day celebration of the Feast of Tabernacles proves that the wilderness wanderings under Moses occupied only eight days."[10]

Sometimes the Sabbath is a full year (cf. Leviticus 25:4). The biological cycle for human beings dictates a twenty-four-hour rest period, for agricultural land, a twelve-month rest period. Since God is not subject to biological cycles, His rest period is completely flexible. Clearly, the emphasis in Exodus 20 is on the pattern of one out of seven, not the literal duration of the days of creation.

Just as the high priests of Israel served "at a sanctuary that is a copy and shadow of what is in heaven" (Hebrews 8:5), the days demarked by the rotation of the earth are copies and shadows of the days distinguished by God in the Genesis creation record. The human and the temporal always are copies and shadows of the divine and the eternal, not vice versa. The seven days of our calendar week simply follow the pattern established by God.

God's "work week" gives us a human-like picture we can grasp. This communication tool is common in the Bible. Scripture frequently speaks of God's hand, His eyes, His arm, even His wings. The context of each of these passages makes it obvious that none of these descriptions is meant to be taken concretely. Rather, each word presents a picture to help us understand spiritual reality about God and His relationship to us.

The difference is *not* literal versus figurative. The difference is between an interpretative method that does not recognize context (including the immediate textual context, the literary genre of the passage, and the broader theological context) and one that does. What I am suggesting here is not a gratuitously figurative or symbolic interpretation of God's creative week, but rather a recognition of anthropomorphic usage that is clearly commonly used elsewhere in Scripture to describe God and His relationship to His creation and His creatures. We need to recognize that the analog of our Sabbath to God's Sabbath does not demand seven twenty-four-hour days. Age-long creation days fit the analogy just as well, if not better.

6. "Death through sin" is not equivalent to physical death. Romans 5:12 says, "Sin entered the world through one man, and death through sin, and in this way death came to all men, because all sinned." Some have interpreted this verse as implying no death of any kind for any creature existed before Adam's sin and, therefore, only a brief time could have transpired between the creation of the first life-forms and Adam's sin.

The proponents of such a view fail to realize that the absence of physical death would pose just as great a problem for three twenty-four-hour days as it would for three billion years. Many species of life cannot survive for even three hours without food, and the mere ingestion of food by animals requires death of at least plants or plant parts.

A rebuttal to this problem suggests that the verse is referring to "soulish" rather than physical death. In the Genesis creation account, soulish creatures (birds and mammals endowed by God with mind, will, and emotions so that they can form relationships with human beings), and spirit creatures (human beings who in addition to the soulish features of birds and mammals are also endowed by God with spirit so that they can form a relationship with God Himself) are distinguished from other animals (invertebrates and lower vertebrates). The difficulty with this adjusted interpretation remains: Are birds and mammals condemned to "death through sin"?

Of all life on the earth, only humans have earned the title "sinner." Only humans can experience "death through sin." Note that the death Adam experienced is carefully qualified in the text as being visited on "all men"—not on plants and animals, just on human beings (Romans 5:12,18-19).

The book of Romans discusses four kinds of death: death to the law, death to sin, physical death, and spiritual death. Romans 5:12 addresses neither physical nor soulish death. It addresses spiritual death. When Adam sinned, he instantly "died," just as God said he would ("In the day that you eat of it, you shall surely die"—Genesis 2:17, NKJV). Yet, he remained alive physically and soulishly (i.e., mentally, volitionally, and emotionally). He died spiritually. He broke his harmonious fellowship with God and introduced the inclination to place one's own way above God's.

In the same manner, it has been established that 1 Corinthians 15:21 ("since death came through a man") also must refer to spiritual death rather than to physical death. As the following two verses in 1 Corinthians explain, "For as in Adam all die, so in Christ all will be made alive. But each in his own turn: Christ, the firstfruits; then, when he comes, those who belong to him" (verses 22-23). Christ grants eternal life through His crucifixion and resurrection, and will give believers indestructible bodies at His return. Christ's crucifixion and resurrection conquered sin and removed the barrier Adam erected between humanity and God. Any person choosing spiritual life in Christ will receive it. Eventually, at Christ's second coming, the eternal spiritual life that the believer in Christ already possesses results in eternal physical life.

My point is that only human beings, spiritual beings, are "made alive in Christ." First Corinthians 15 refers only to those creatures who experience sin and desire to be delivered from sin. This excludes all species of life on the earth except humans. Therefore, just as in Romans 5, no reason is found to deny physical death for nonhuman life previous to Adam's sin.

Genesis 3 records that *after* Adam and Eve died (spiritually) through sin, God sent an angel to block their access to the tree of life. Apparently Adam and Eve had the potential for eternal physical life before *and* after sinning against God. Knowing that eternal physical life in their newly acquired sinful condition ultimately would be disastrous for them and their descendants, God barred their access to it. God would not allow His plan to be thwarted. Physical death for humans became a blessing designed to restrain the spread of evil and make way for the redemption of willing men and women.[11]

One point of concern remains. Some people think that the death of plants and animals before Adam's sin ascribes evil to the Creator. I have met men and women who deny that a God of love could be responsible for carnivorous behavior. They believe that carnivorous activity must be the result of sin and not of God's design.

Biologists, physicists, and engineers with whom I have discussed this concern offer this perspective: An organism's place in the food chain determines its capacity for efficient work. The differences in daily activity between creatures that consume low-calorie leaves and those that consume high-calorie seeds, and between those that consume seeds and those that consume animals are dramatic. Elephants, for example, are vegetarians and, even though they are large (thus experiencing less loss of heat), must spend more than half their waking hours harvesting and eating, and they cannot do any hopping or jumping. The destruction they wreak on their environment in attempting to devour sufficient calories results in the death of many plants and smaller animals, arguably more death than is caused by large carnivores.

Considering how creatures convert chemical energy into kinetic energy, we can say that carnivorous activity results from the laws of thermodynamics, not from sin. Large, active, agile land animals either must spend virtually all their waking hours grazing, drinking, or digesting or they must consume meat. And I don't think we should hastily label the thermodynamic laws as evil. Without them, life in this universe would be impossible. (See item 8 on decay, pages 65-66.)

There's an obvious emotional side to this matter of killing and eating animals. We tend to anthropomorphize and thus distort the suffering of animals. But even plants suffer when they are eaten. They experience bleeding, bruising, scarring, and death. Why is the suffering of plants acceptable and not that of animals? Consider, too, how little concern we feel over the death of insects. Why?

Obviously, the difference between the physical death of a spirit creature and the death of any other creature is in some ways profound. Because of the soulish characteristics of certain animals, especially those we domesticate and make pets of, we tend to see them as more like persons. Let us remind ourselves that they are not and that we cannot realistically compare the suffering and death of animals to the suffering and death of humans.

Again, I am not disputing that God could have done

things differently. But our job as thinking people, whether scientists or theologians, is not to question God's motives or His ways but rather to determine what, in fact, He has done and is doing. As explained in section 8 (page 68), God has so designed His creation that willing humans can be led forward into the new creation (Revelation 21). A relatively brief and limited amount of suffering by us and the entire universe brings about a reward so great that none of us can even imagine how wonderful it will be (1 Corinthians 2:9).

7. *Bloodshed before Adam's sin does not alter the doctrine of atonement.* Hebrews 9:22 says, "In fact, the law requires that nearly everything be cleansed with blood, and without the shedding of blood there is no forgiveness." Ken Ham of the Institute for Creation Research interprets the verse this way, "The basis of the Gospel message is that God brought in death and bloodshed because of sin."[12] As he explains, "If death and bloodshed of animals (or man) existed before Adam sinned, then the whole basis of atonement—the basis of redemption—is destroyed."[13]

While it is true that there is no remission of sin without the shedding of blood, Christ's blood, it does not necessarily follow that *all* shed blood is for the remission of sin. (To say there could have been no bloodshed before sin is to make the same exegetical error as made by those who claim there were no rainstorms or rainbows before the Genesis flood.)

Hebrews 10:1-4 explains that the blood of animal sacrifices *will not take away sin.* The sacrificial killing of animals was a physical picture of the spiritual death caused by sin, which necessitated the death of a substitute to make atonement, as well as a foreshadowing of the ultimate, efficacious sacrifice that God Himself would one day provide. Since the penalty for sin is spiritual death, no animal sacrifice could ever atone for sin. The crime is spiritual. Thus the atonement had to be made by a spiritual Being.

The spilling of blood before Adam's sin in no way affects or detracts from the doctrine of atonement. Upholding that central doctrine in no way demands a creation scenario in which none of God's creatures received a scratch or other blood-letting wound before Adam and Eve sinned. Incidentally, experiencing no bloodshed is just as big a problem for animal life existing for forty-eight hours as it would be for animal life existing for millions of years. Even in an ideal natural environment animals would be constantly scratched, pricked, bruised, and even killed by accidental events and each other.

8. The creation has been subject to "its bondage of decay" since its beginning. Romans 8:20-22 describes this bondage:

> For the creation was subjected to frustration, not by its own choice, but by the will of the one who subjected it, in hope that the creation itself will be liberated from its bondage to decay and brought into the glorious freedom of the children of God. We know that the whole creation has been groaning as in the pains of childbirth right up to the present time.

These words have been interpreted by some to imply that Adam's sin ushered into the creation all manner of natural decay, including pain and death. They assume that the law of entropy, which describes the decreasing order in the universe, did not take effect until Adam and Eve sinned. Based on this assumption, the time between the universe's creation and Adam and Eve's fall must be brief to explain why the physical evidence shows no period when decay and death were not in operation.

This appeal fails on several counts. While it is obvious that freedom from decay, suffering, and pain could not possibly extend through billions of years, it is less obvious, but equally certain, that it could not last for even one twenty-four-hour day. Without decay, work (at least in the universe God designed) would be impossible (see box, page 66). Without work, physical life would be impossible, for work is essential to breathing, circulating blood, contracting muscles, digesting food—virtually all life-sustaining processes. And life did exist, according to Genesis 1, at least from the third creation day. And Adam was working, tending the Garden of Eden (Genesis 2:15), before he sinned. Thus Romans 8:20-22 could not imply that Adam's sin inaugurated the decay process.

Decay and Work

The second law of thermodynamics states that heat will flow from hot bodies to cold bodies. A consequence of this direction of heat flow is that, as time proceeds, the universe becomes progressively more mixed or disordered. This increasing disorder, with time, is the principle of decay, also termed "entropy."

But in the process of increasing decay lies the potential to perform work. Because of the principle of pervasive decay, heat energy can be transformed into mechanical energy (or work) if the heat flow is channeled through an engine.[14] The amount of heat energy that can be so transformed into work is proportional to the difference between the temperature of the hot body and the temperature of the cold body divided by the temperature of the hot body (temperatures measured relative to absolute zero).

For organisms, the temperature difference between the hot and cold bodies must be small enough to preserve the lives of the organisms. Thus the work efficiencies are very low. In any case, given the laws of physics that God ordained for the universe, without the process of decay, no work at all would be possible and, therefore, life would be impossible.

Actually, Romans 8 explicitly indicates only when the bondage to decay will end. It says little about when it first began. I say little because the repeated references to "the creation" and "the whole creation" (verse 22) seem to imply the entire creation. The equations of general relativity indicate that the entire creation includes not only all the matter and energy in the universe but also the space-time dimensions (length, width, height, and time) of the universe.[15] This, in turn, would imply that the process of decay has been in effect since the universe was created.

The text might refer, as well, to another kind of decay: the disorder in people's life and environment that has resulted from rebellion against God. In Genesis 1:28, God commanded us to tend the environment. But, because we sinned, the environment has been ruined. The human effect on the environment is roughly analogous to the results of sending a two-year-old child to tidy up a closet. Left alone, the closet will become less tidy due to the natural tendency toward decay and disorder. Typically, though, that two-year-old will greatly speed up the decay and disorder process. Isaiah 24:5 describes the devastation of the planet that results from the insubordination of human beings to God.

Just as one must wait for the two-year-old child to grow up a little before expecting him to help tidy up a closet, so, too, the creation waits for the human race to experience the results of God's conquering the sin problem.

Those who interpret Romans 8 as I do are said to place science above the Bible and to stretch the text beyond reasonable limits to accommodate science.[16-18] But can such a charge apply to third-century church leader Origen (AD 185–254)? The title he gave to chapter V, book III of *On First Principles* is this: "That the world is originated and subject to decay, since it took its beginning in time." Origen in that chapter explains his interpretation of Romans 8:20-22. He says it implies that decay has been in effect in the natural world since the creation of the universe.[19] Because he preceded by hundreds of years the scientific discovery of the laws of thermodynamics and entropy (which include the principle of decay), it seems unreasonable to accuse him of submitting to the pressure of the scientific community.

If we turn back to the passage recounting God's

response to Adam and Eve's sin, we see evidence that physical pain—closely connected with decay—must have existed before the Fall. In Genesis 3:16, God says to Eve, "I will greatly increase [or multiply] your pains in childbearing." He does not say "introduce." He says "increase" or "multiply," implying there would have been pain in any case. Perhaps it is not incidental that the Romans 8 passage uses the analogy of birth pangs.

Why Did God Choose the Laws of Physics?

Speculation on why God set the physical laws as He did is beyond our human capacity to comprehend: "As the heavens are higher than the earth, so are my ways higher than your ways and my thoughts than your thoughts," declares the Lord (Isaiah 55:9). But we do know the physical laws governing the universe were designed by God to accomplish His purposes, one of which is quickly to conquer evil.[20] These laws necessarily involve decay processes. But once God completes His conquest of evil—ultimately at a future event called the great white throne judgment (Revelation 20:11-15)—the need for these laws will disappear. Indeed, it is awesome to consider that God created as He did, for billions of years, so that our time of suffering can be kept brief.

The laws of physics will be replaced right after the great white throne judgment, according to Revelation 21, by an entirely new and different set of physical laws (see pages 67-70). Thus, the liberation of the whole creation from the bondage to decay awaits the final victory over Satan and the glorification of all of God's children.

Though we all dislike pain, we have good reasons to be grateful for it. Pain is essential for our safety and survival. Thanks to our nervous system and its quick pain response, we are protected from many dangers of our environment.

An engineer friend was once so absorbed in an electronics project that he inadvertantly rested his hand on the heating element of a nearby soldering iron. Not until he smelled smoke did he realize that his hand was burning. At that point he wished his pain sensors had been more effective! It appears that God has given us enough pain to protect us from harm but not so much as to make life continually unbearable for all of us.

In the context of the Garden of Eden, one consequence of the introduction of sin was to increase the risk of harm for Adam and Eve, and hence their need for an increase in sensitivity to pain. I believe Adam and Eve had intact nervous systems before they sinned. Their sense of touch would have been a source of pleasure, discovery, and protection in the garden. Can we really imagine life in this universe without the sense of touch?

While the sin we human beings commit causes us all naturally to react negatively to decay, work, physical death, pain, and suffering, and while ultimately all this is somehow tied into God's plan to conquer sin permanently, there is nothing in Scripture that compels us to conclude that none of these entities existed before Adam's first act of rebellion against God. On the other hand, God's revelation through nature provides overwhelming evidence that all these aspects indeed did exist for a long time period previous to God's creating Adam (see chapters 9–10, pages 91-118).

9. God's rest (cessation) from creating will someday end, and He will create again. According to Revelation 21, once God permanently conquers evil, this present universe will be replaced by a brand-new one. Though God has not physically created since He formed Eve, His Sabbath day of rest is scheduled to end. With evil no longer a factor, the purpose for our universe will have been fulfilled. Therefore, God will remove from existence this universe with its laws of physics. He will replace it with new heavens, a new earth, and a new Jerusalem, with laws of physics designed to make possible our eternal life and rewards in His presence.

Evidence that the laws of physics in the new creation

will be different comes, for example, from the description of the new Jerusalem. The dimensions of the city—a 1,500-mile cube—would be physically impossible in our universe (gravity would cause an object larger than a few hundred miles across to collapse into a sphere). The significant point, however, is that the creation week described in Genesis 1 is only the beginning. God will create again. His period of rest or cessation from creating, His Sabbath day, has a definite beginning point in the past (right after the creation of Eve) and an ending point in the future (when God creates the new heavens and earth). Thousands of years are passing between this beginning and ending. The parallel structure in the description of the seven Genesis creation days suggests, then, that the other days are also longer than twenty-four hours.

10. God is no less powerful for taking more than 144 hours to create. Some creationists have expressed the idea that a cosmic creation date of billions of years ago depreciates the omnipotence of God. Just as the runner who covers a mile in four minutes must be stronger than the one who requires ten minutes, it is presumed that a God who takes billions of years to create must be weaker than a God who takes only six twenty-four-hour days.

Two fallacies underlie this line of reasoning. One is that God's creating in six twenty-four-hour days proves Him all-powerful. Not so. Even that time frame is too long. For that matter, six nanoseconds would be too long. God would have created everything in one immeasurable instant if time were a measure of His power. The second fallacy is that an all-powerful God is under compulsion to exercise all His power all the time. Just as a man capable of running a four-minute mile has the option to take more time, so God can choose whatever time frame He pleases for whatever He does.

God's deliberate action is emphasized by the apostle Peter in 2 Peter 3:9—"The Lord is not slow in keeping his promise, as some understand slowness." The rushing and hyperactivity characteristic of modern society in no way reflect the Creator. He is never anxious, always patient, and always willing to trade the temporal for the eternal.

Throughout the biblical narratives, we see God restraining His full power. This restraint is clearly visible in the actions of Jesus Christ. He steadfastly resisted pressure to unleash the full force of His divine power, choosing instead to achieve a higher goal.

Certainly God has His reasons for the time scale He chose. If we cannot comprehend all His reasons, we still have no basis for second-guessing Him. He is God, and His ways and thoughts are above ours. Perhaps the time scale He chose fits into His strategy for conquering evil. Perhaps He is using a certain time scale to teach something to human beings or to the angels. Perhaps . . . no matter how much we learn, we will never know the totality of God's mind.

Conclusion

Allow me to add one final consideration both theological and personal. In the great commission (Matthew 28:19, Luke 24:47), Jesus commands His followers to make disciples of all nations. The Greek word for nation, *ethnos*, refers to a group of people associated with each other by some common characteristics or experiences.[21] The host of the redeemed pictured in Revelation 7 comes from "every nation, tribe, people, and language." In 1 Corinthians 1:26, Paul says that not many believers are from the group considered "wise" and "influential" by the standards of the world. He says "not many" rather than not any. Apparently, at least a few of the world's "wise and influential," which I believe must include some intellectuals and other leaders, give their lives to Jesus Christ.

I see the community of scientists, including astronomers and astrophysicists, as an *ethnos*. God calls us to reach out to them as He does to every other group on the planet. And though He warns that the childlike simplicity of trusting in Jesus will be a stumbling block for many, we have unwittingly placed another barrier in their path: the dogma of a few-thousand-year-old earth. I cannot imagine a notion more offensive to this group. Since all of their research convinces them that the universe they are studying is real, they understandably resist embracing the belief that it is all a mirage (see pages 91-102 and 126-133).

When young-earth creationists claim (as did Russell Akridge[22] among others) that the worldwide community of secular astrophysicists and astronomers are banded together in a God-hating conspiracy to deceive the public about the creation date, the offense is driven deeper. Given the tendency toward independence and nonconformity among them, it's absurd to suggest that tens of thousands of them would or could unanimously carry out a plot through four decades to bamboozle the public. Another explanation must exist for their strong and united confidence in the creation date (as billions of years ago) for the universe and the earth.

I believe God wants us to remove the artificial stumbling block so that attention can be focused on the central issue of salvation in Christ. As I have attempted to show, the theological case supporting a young earth and a twenty-four-hour creation day is largely untenable under close scrutiny. History reveals, however, the driving force behind this theological artifice: It is fear rather than fact. Fear says long creation days somehow accommodate the Darwinian claim that by strictly natural processes operating over four billion years, life arose from a primordial soup and evolved on its own into human beings. If there were any foundation to this fear, then the reaction of young-earth creationists would be understandable. But the question must be asked: Is this fear well founded? Do long creation days and an old earth and universe really make room for naturalistic evolution? The answer is a resounding no, as the next chapter makes clear.

CHAPTER SEVEN

Do Long Creation Days Imply Evolution?

A Canadian university professor with whom I correspond refers to evolution as the Christian *E*-word, a word so emotionally charged that its mere mention sets off fire alarms in people's heads. No wonder acceptance of the antiquity of the universe, the earth, and life so often draws a blast.

Christians have been taught what early fundamentalists — and their opponents — believed, that to accept a long creation time scale is tantamount to accepting the self-assembly of molecules into humans (via the monkeys). Heightening this issue are the Genesis flood doctrines of many modern young-earth creationists. Since they believe that all of today's land animals are descended from the creatures on Noah's ark, and since they recognize the ark as too small and the caretakers on board too few to preserve all the land animals on the earth today, they conclude Noah took two of every order, genus, or subgenus rather than two of every species. The many species of today are presumed to arise through biological evolution from the orders and genera on Noah's ark![1] Extrapolating such rapid biological evolution over a few billion years seems to imply little need for God beyond the first life-forms or the first members of a phylum.

Before addressing the capabilities of biological evolutionary processes, it is helpful to clear away some of the emotion surrounding the offensive term, *evolution*.

Confused Definitions

In its ordinary usage among scientists and non-scientists alike, especially among physical scientists, *evolution* simply mea..s "change with respect to time." The time can be short or long. The change can be small or great and more or less gradual. The cause can be intelligent or nonintelligent. By this definition, we could say that Genesis 1 describes evolution, for it describes change in the realm of nature with respect to time, however long or short that time.

Because this meaning of evolution is the one they have in mind, scientists become perplexed at the Christian's typical reaction to the term. Scientists cannot comprehend why anyone would take exception. The problem is that the Christian is responding to an entirely different definition.

To most Christians, the definition is usually the narrow biological one: the theory that all species developed from earlier forms. The dictionary does not add the phrase, "without divine miraculous intervention," but people, Christians and others, assume it's there. Nor does the definition include any comment about the origin of life, but for many people the word *evolution* implies that natural processes alone produced the gigantic leap from inorganic to organic.

Even when this particular meaning is the one intended, a crucial question must be asked, Do long creation days provide sufficient time for life to originate on its own and to develop from simple to more and more complex on its own?

Origin-of-Life Possibilities

The naturalist's problem is bridging the gap between relatively simple inorganic systems and vastly more complex self-reproducing organic systems. The difference between an aqueous solution containing a few amino acids and other prebiotic molecules and the simplest living cell is enormous. (The first organic entity appearing in the fossil record is a fully formed cell. Biologists do not suggest that an organic entity any simpler than a cell could survive independently.)

Years ago, molecular biologist Harold Morowitz calculated the distance between the inorganic and organic worlds. If one were to take the simplest living cell and break every chemical bond within it, the odds that the cell would reassemble under ideal conditions (the best possible chemical conditions where no foreign substances would be permitted to intrude nor any of the needed substances permitted to leave) would be one chance in $10^{100,000,000,000}$.[2]

With odds as remote as 1 in $10^{100,000,000,000}$, the creation time-scale issue becomes irrelevant. Whether the earth has been around for ten seconds, ten thousand years, or ten billion years makes no difference. Nor does the size of the universe matter. If all the material in the visible universe were converted into the building blocks of life (amino acids and nucleotides), and if assembly of these blocks were attempted once a microsecond for the entire age of the universe (about 17 billion years or 5×10^{17} seconds), the number of opportunities to form a living entity, 10^{84}, is so enormously smaller than the number required to give a reaonable probability of success, $10^{100,000,000,000}$, as to make no difference at all in the likelihood of the spontaneous formation of life. Given these numbers, how absurd for Christians to argue about a mere factor of 10^6 (the difference between a universe created ten thousand years ago compared to 10 billion years ago)!

Actually, the odds are worse. Morowitz assumed the presence of only bioactive building blocks. In the real world nonbioactive building blocks are mixed in with the bioactive ones. Only twenty of the more than eighty naturally occurring amino acids are bioactive and only those with the hydrogen atom on the left side (about half the amino acids) can be used in biological systems. Morowitz also assumed that only constructive chemical processes would operate. Under natural conditions, destructive chemical processes operate at least as frequently as constructive ones.

Not every building block in the molecular chains within living cells must fit strictly in sequence. Some substitutions are permissible. But this flexibility adds no substantial help to the naturalists' argument for the origin of life.[3-5]

Additional Complications

Two more problems thwart the idea of prebiotic molecules assembling themselves into living cells. One is the irrational assumption of prebiotic molecules arriving without divine design. Recent research shows that at least twenty-five different characteristics of the universe must be exquisitely fine-tuned for life's essential building blocks to exist.[6] In several cases the degree of fine-tuning exceeds one part in 10^{37}. This fine-tuning far exceeds anything humans have been able to achieve—even with advanced technology—in our most magnificent projects. We can conclude only that the Cause of the building blocks of life is unimaginably intelligent, creative, capable, and caring. If the involvement of a Creator is necessary to explain the crafting of the simplest building blocks of life, how much more would He be needed to explain the design and assembly of living organisms?

The second problem lies in false assumptions about the benefit of time and durability of the building blocks. To illustrate, compare essential-for-life molecules with the parts of a watch. In the absence of friction and erosion, it would be almost conceivable for watch parts loosely placed in a shoe box to self-assemble bit by bit into a finished watch under careful, *gentle* shaking of the box. Careful, because the shaking must be stopped at exactly the moment when the parts come together, since subsequent shaking would lead quickly to the disassembly of the watch parts. This precise timing, in itself, requires an intelligent "box shaker."

I say the shaking must be stopped quickly because at each point in the assembly sequence, under random shaking of the box, the probability would be higher for disassembly of the watch parts than for assembly. As any watchmaker will testify, piecing together the parts of a quality timepiece takes intense concentration and exquisite, purposeful manipulation. Given the far higher probability of disassembly than of assembly, it is arguable at what point time becomes a hindrance rather than a help in the random assembly of parts into a finished watch. Likewise it is arguable at what point time turns against the chances for strictly natural assembly of building blocks into living organisms.

Also, friction and erosion cannot be ignored. In the real world—organic and inorganic—they continually occur. In the watch analogy, continuous shaking of the box will turn the gears and sprockets into dust long before they assemble themselves into a finished watch. The durability of the watch parts falls far short of the random-assembly time. In the case of proteins, DNA and RNA molecules, their breakdown into simpler molecules or into nonfunctioning molecules would occur far more quickly than would their random self-assembly from simpler molecules into living organisms, or even into the component proteins, DNA, and RNA.

The most recent scientific determination of the maximum time it took for the first life-form to originate on the earth is 10 million years.[7] The 10 million years might as well be ten nanoseconds, for such a time span is, by far, inadequate for self-assembly of atoms into organisms.

From Primordial Life to Humankind

Another myth has long held sway in evolutionary biology, a myth that says the 3.8 billion years between the first life-form on the earth and the first humans is adequate time for single-celled creatures to transform themselves into human beings. The basis for the myth is twofold:

1. The mechanism of natural selection has been observed under field conditions and in controlled breeding experiments to produce from a single species in just a few centuries two sets of individuals so distinct from one another that they cannot successfully mate to produce survivable, fertile progeny. Thus, one species (loosely defined) apparently has split into two.
2. The mechanism of successive mutations has been observed under field conditions and in laboratory experiments to produce offspring that in just a few decades can supplant the non-mutated members of the species. Thus, one species changes into another.

Ignoring the limitations on these two mechanisms, a person might presume that several billion years worth of extrapolation might explain much, if not all, of the fossil record details. Unfortunately the limitations are much too severe to support a strictly natural interpretation.

Limitations on Natural Selection

The canine species provides a helpful example of how far natural selection can and cannot go. Through decades of selective breeding wild dogs have become hundreds of distinct breeds. Today we see teacup poodles no bigger than a person's hand and great danes nearly the size of a pony. Obviously, a male teacup poodle is physically unable to mate successfully with a female great dane.

If a common definition of a species (a class of creatures that can mate and produce fertile offspring) is used, the dog species has developed into more than one species. But consider the impact of that "speciation." Both teacup poodles and great danes are fragile in terms of life expectancy and survivability. If they were forced to fend for themselves in the wild, they would rapidly become extinct. The farther we breed the progeny away from the norm (or mean) of the species, the less survivable the progeny become. Though to breed a dog even smaller than a teacup poodle may be possible, breeders would eventually bump against the limits of natural selection. The smaller the dog, the more difficult to keep it alive even in the protection of our homes.

Ironically, natural selection usually argues for stasis rather than for change.[8] In the case of dogs, if we remove all the barriers separating different breeds and allow the breeds to mingle freely in the wild, within relatively few generations the progeny would revert back to the mean.

Where natural selection does work to change a species, the change is minor. We humans are about half a foot taller and can see better than our ancestors of millenia ago. Most of this change can be attributed to improved diet. Some is the result of natural selection—e.g., people with clearer eyesight are better able to dodge spears and other hazards. The contributions of natural selection to the human species remain so tiny, however, as to prove inconsequential for explaining the differences between humans and any other species, including the apes.

For some species, even this possibility for slight change does not exist. Natural selection is founded on the principle that a species will overpopulate to such a degree that only the fittest survive. But not all species overpopulate. Many species of birds, for example, reduce their egg production in direct proportion to the supply of food. Their populations are not limited by starvation and predation but rather by instinctively controlled breeding.

Limitations on Mutational Change

In the process of natural selection, one gene may be chosen over another. But in mutations (chemical changes in complex molecules induced by radiation and other environmental stresses), the chemical structure of the gene itself is changed. Therefore, mutations carry the potential for producing dramatic changes in the characteristics of a species. These changes, however, are limited by the generation time span and the population size of the species.

Mutations occur only rarely. Typically only one individual in a million will experience a mutation. Most nonlethal mutations are neutral. That is, they have no effect on the characteristics of the progeny carrying the change. Of the remaining mutations, the majority are harmful to the species. The ratio of harmful to favorable mutations measures between ten thousand to one and a million to one.

With favorable mutation rates as low as one per 10 billion individuals or lower, most species cannot mutate rapidly enough to adapt to severe environmental stresses. The likelihood for extinction far exceeds the likelihood for mutating into a new, survivable species. The exceptions are species with huge populations and short generations. Species with a quadrillion individuals (or more) and a life cycle of three months or less stand a reasonable chance of propagating a sufficient number of favorable mutations to adapt to minor environmental challenges. Ants, termites, bacteria, and viruses fall into this category. For the vast majority of species, however, mutations are destructive. Virtually all will go extinct long before they could change successfully via mutation. For all species, nothing like the development of new organs falls within the range of reasonable probability.

One response of evolutionary biologists to this dilemma is to hypothesize periods in Earth's history during which the mutation rate greatly exceeded one per million individuals. However, circumstances generating such a high mutation rate would also threaten the survival of all progeny, both mutated and unmutated. Therefore, the increased mutation rate would be counterbalanced, if not vastly overbalanced, by a decreased population and decreased probability that survivors will successfully reproduce and provide for the needs of their offspring.

Conclusion

Interpreting the Genesis creation days as tens of millions or even hundreds of millions of Earth years in no way lends support to evolutionism. These time frames would be too brief by countless orders of magnitude for simple life to arise and become complex by natural processes.

The fear expressed by many devout Christians that long creation days grease a slide into the tenets of naturalistic evolution (belief that all life arises from natural processes only) or theistic evolution (belief that God creates only through His control of the natural processes, never independent of them) has no scientific foundation. It is a little known fact that a sizable proportion of biology research fellows, professors, and graduate students at leading institutions are Bible-believing Christians who deny the neo-Darwinist hypotheses of molecules to primordial life and primordial life to humans through natural processes alone.[9]

CHAPTER EIGHT

Do Long Creation Days Imperil Faith and Morality?

Recently a national news publication, *Insight on the News,* featured a report on the political stance of the religious right. It concluded with this comment:

> The religious right . . . is comfortable using government power to legislate morality on issues such as homosexuality and creationism.[1]

Here we see a reflection of how the public views the Christian agenda. Secularists fear that we will push through laws enforcing our moral beliefs about abortion, homosexuality, *and* young-universe creationism. This perception of creationism as a moral issue helps explain why emotions run so high when the age of the universe and the earth comes into discussion. But how valid is this categorization?

Linking Long Creation Days to Immorality

Unfortunately a large segment of the Christian community has been taught to equate acceptance of an old universe with a slide into immorality. The most vocal and articulate promoters of this connection come from the Institute for Creation Research (ICR) and the Bible-Science Association (BSA).

The equation of old-universe, old-earth views with immorality begins with the idea that the old-earth concept promotes evolutionism. Henry Morris, founder and president of the ICR, states the link:

The continued insistence on an ancient earth is purely
because of the philosophic necessity to justify evolution
and the pantheistic religion of eternal matter.[2]

Morris's son John, also of the ICR, echoes his father's words:

The old earth is an integral component of evolutionary
ideas. . . . The old earth concept is a requisite of evolutionism.[3]

To John Morris evolutionism is "an unmitigated evil," the
philosophical root of "fascism, racism, Marxism, social Darwinism, and imperialism." In his view, the "modern ills of
promiscuity, homosexuality, abortion, humanism, new-age
pantheism, etc.," all "flower from the same evil root."[4]

In case any Christian fails to recognize the theorem, old-
earth beliefs = evolutionism, evolutionism = unmitigated
evil, therefore, old-earth beliefs = unmitigated evil. Morris
calls the old-earth view "anti-Biblical" and "anti-theistic,"
and adds that "there can be no justification for a Christian
adopting the old-earth concept." He ends one article with a
special exhortation to Christian leaders who "hold and perhaps teach the old-earth concept knowledgeably" to "aban-
don their compromise of Scripture" and to "eschew the evils
of a failed scientific theory."[5]

Henry Morris began to voice these opinions long before
his son did. In a book entitled *The Long War Against God,* the
elder Morris comments on social disintegration:

The failure of Bible-believing Christian churches and
schools to aggressively defend and promote true biblical
creationism [i.e., young-earth creationism] is a major
cause of the takeover by evolutionary humanism of our
entire society. . . . The modern widespread rebellion
against God's commandments related to the family is
conditional upon the prior rejection of his creation activity and record thereof.[6]

In an earlier article he made this charge:

> If it were not for the continued apathetic and compromising attitude of Christian theologians and other intellectuals on this vital doctrine of recent creation, evolutionary humanism would long since have been exposed and defeated.[7]

Hammering his point repeatedly, Morris calls progressive creationism (including the belief that God instantly performs miracles of creation on many different occasions over long time periods) "a compromise with the enemy."[8] In fact, he labels progressive creationism with its day-age theory the worst of all options, for it "compounds the offense [of evolutionism] by making God have to redirect and recharge everything at intervals."[9] He reasons, "The very concept of the geological ages implies divine confusion and cruelty."[10]

Strong words reflect strong feelings. But, as I mentioned in the previous chapter (see page 73), these feelings partly spring from the belief on the part of many young-earth creationists that natural biological evolutionary processes really do work. This leads to a tremendous irony. Such creationists brand day-age proponents, like myself, who deny any significant biological evolution over time scales long or short, as evolutionists, while they themselves seem to concede substantial biological evolution over very short time scales.

Some Christians take John Morris's theorem a step further: Since old-earth beliefs = unmitigated evil, then old-earth proponents = evil people. The Bible-Science Association in *Bible Science News* expressed outrage that the story of my commitment to Christ was published in a Christian magazine. Twice they termed me "dangerous," adding that I am "not an orthodox Christian," and claiming that I reject Christ's atonement.[11] Ken Ham of the ICR makes similarly severe charges against old-earth creationists. In an article, he berated Christian leaders who "believe that God created various groups of animals and plants throughout the supposed millions of years of the history of life, and that then He created Adam and Eve."[12] He issued this warning:

> It is these leaders who affect so many people with their persuasive arguments of whom we have to be aware.
> . . . Satan will use people with clever words who can sound scientific, to undermine this foundation. Such people, I believe, are described in Matthew 7:15: "Beware of false prophets, which come to you in sheep's clothing, but inwardly they are ravening wolves."[13]

Linking Long Creation Days to Apostasy

In attacking the old-earth, old-universe view, the Institute for Creation Research and the Bible-Science Association not only raise their scepter against the "unmitigated evil" of evolutionism, they also sound the alarm against apostasy, a departure from the true Christian faith. They carry another torch, upholding twenty-four-hour creation days and recent creation dates as essential requirements for salvation. Those who believe God created over billions of years are said to deny the fundamental doctrines of the Christian faith.

John Morris wrote that billions of years of new species appearing and old species becoming extinct is "inconsistent with God's omnipotence, omniscience, purposiveness, loving nature and even His grace."[14] He also claims the old-earth view negates the doctrine of Christ's atonement for sins to give believers eternal life:

> In this [old-earth] view, death is *not* the penalty for sin, for it preceded man and his sin. But if death is not the penalty for sin, then the death of Jesus Christ did not pay that penalty, nor did His resurrection from the dead provide eternal life.[15]

Ken Ham's view is that the old-earth view of creation "destroys the basis of the Gospel message" and "the message of redemption."[16] The Bible-Science Association agrees:

> [Old-earth] theology denies the central teaching of
> Christianity . . . and rejects the connection that Scripture
> establishes between sin, death, and Christ's atonement.
> . . . In [this] theology death is natural. Death was a
> reality for millions of years before man ever arrived to
> sin. This leaves Christ's death on the cross as, at best,
> well-meaning, but beside the point.[17]

An old-earth perspective is also depicted as a fundamental challenge to the authority of the Bible. Referring to
Christians who accept "billions of years," Ham says, "They
have put man in judgment of God. *Man* becomes the authority." He continues with this emotional appeal: "For me to
accept an old age (billions of years) for the earth is to accept
that fallible man's fallible methods are in authority over
God's infallible Word. I can't do that!"[18]

Russell Humphreys, an adjunct professor of physics for
the ICR, equates old-earth creationism with a sadistic God
and a denial of the second coming of Christ.[19] Henry and
John Morris claim that the ministries of old-earth creationists
do not lead to soul-winning or spiritual growth.[20]

These spokesmen have widely and deeply influenced
the beliefs of many Christians (not to mention observers of
Christians) around the world. They seem to believe sincerely
that these foundational doctrines of the Christian faith are
destroyed in the acknowledgment that the universe and the
earth may be older than thousands of years. No wonder they
and those they have influenced show so little restraint in
branding old-earth creationists as apostates, deceivers,
underminers of the faith, false prophets, and purveyors of
sin and evil.

Polarizing Impact

By attempting to link belief in long creation days with homosexuality, abortion, promiscuity, pantheism, Marxism, racism, imperialism, fascism, social Darwinism, unmitigated
evil, scriptural compromise, denial of Christ's atonement

and the gift of eternal life, and disinterest in soul-winning and spiritual growth, these young-earth creationists have prepared Christians to respond with hatred and contempt toward old-earth creationists. In reviling what old-earth creationists say, many Christians' ears and minds are closed. They see no need to hear or weigh any evidences. There's no openness to rethinking, for too much is at stake. Only complete repentance from old-earth beliefs will do.

Frankly, given the supposed linkages, this response is understandable. It is difficult to remain dispassionate when facing purveyors of evil and apostasy, especially purveyors who call themselves Christians. This polarization leads to emotion-charged confrontations.

One radio talk-show host received a vigorous scolding from a caller for permitting me to speak on the air. The caller was sure I was incorrect about astronomy, though he had never studied the subject. He cared nothing that I was on the pastoral staff of an evangelical church known for its outreach and growth. All that mattered to him was that I be denied the opportunity to speak because he thought I might confuse and harm someone's faith. I knew he could not be responding to me, personally, but rather to his solidly reinforced presumptions about me.

Another encounter took place near the Oakridge Nuclear Facility in Tennessee, where I spoke on scientific evidences for the God of the Bible. With the room full of research physicists, I focused on proofs from physics and astronomy for a transcendent, personal, and caring Creator. Unknown to me and the meeting's organizers, a carload of young-universe proponents had driven for four-and-a-half hours to make a spectacle of me at this gathering. When the question period opened they took over, attempting first to take apart my physics and astronomy data. They were furious that the scientists in the room would not join them in refuting my science. So blinded were they by their indoctrination regarding the evils of belief in the antiquity of the universe that they disrupted a meeting intended to introduce people to personal faith in Jesus Christ (including His sacrifice to atone for our sin).

Perhaps some readers are aware of my attempted dialogue with Duane Gish (of the ICR) on Dr. James Dobson's "Focus on the Family" radio broadcast.[21] Our subject was the age of the universe, but it received little attention. Primarily, Dr. Gish gave *his* account of my Christian and scientific beliefs. He remained resolutely on this tack against my own and Dr. Dobson's objections. With Morris's theorem so deeply ingrained, Dr. Gish could not hear my words nor accept that I believe anything other than evolutionism and aberrant Christian doctrines.

Severing the False Link to Immorality

I see no hope of meaningful dialogue and reconciliation among Christians on the time-scale issue until the supposed link between old-earth creationism and immorality is broken. People must see proof that John Morris's theorem is not true.

An important preface to the dismantling of the theorem, however, is public praise for the tireless efforts of young-earth creationists against the spread of immorality and nonChristian values. They rightfully deserve credit for their commitment, courage, and outspokenness in this cause.

As for the theorem, the previous chapter demonstrates the falsehood of the first statement, old-earth = evolutionism. If the first statement breaks down, the entire theorem falls apart. But I believe there's a need to challenge the second statement also, that evolutionism = unmitigated evil. It may come from or lead to rejection of God's truth, but many of its adherents simply have not yet thought through the implications of what they've been taught. Most Darwinists and evolutionists I've met are inconsistent in the application of what they profess to believe about life's origin and development. They do not manifest the evils that John Morris suggests. I believe God calls us to treat them as potential converts, not as enemies to be attacked and destroyed. As the apostle Paul points out in 1 Corinthians 6:9-11, there is hope even for those who are caught up in evil. Grace, mercy, and truth are what they need. Hate and contempt should be expressed toward sin but not toward the sinner, for we have all sinned.

An equally important idea to challenge is Henry Morris's assertion that "an omniscient God could devise a better process of creation than the random, wasteful, inefficient trial-and-error charade of the so-called geological ages," and that "a loving merciful God would never be guilty of a creative process that would involve the suffering and death of multitudes of innocent animals."[22]

If these assertions are true, what can we say of the present era? God could do much right now to reduce our suffering. But a loving, merciful God allows the epitome of His creation—humankind—to suffer discomfort, illness, injury, and death. God even calls the death of His saints precious (Psalm 116:15). Could it be that God's purposes are somehow fulfilled through our experiencing the "random, wasteful, inefficiencies" of the natural realm He created?

Were conditions significantly different in the past? Is the suffering and death of grasses, leaves, and protozoa that must have occurred before Adam and Eve sinned (even in Morris's system of theology) totally tragic, meaningless, and without any purpose?

While it's true that an omniscient God could have devised a different kind of creation, we would be arrogant to decide that God "could devise a better process of creation." As I wrote in chapter 6 (pages 53-72), given God's grand plans and goals for the new creation, the new heavens, and the new earth (Revelation 21), the groanings experienced by the present creation (Romans 8:18-25) may represent a brief but essential experience along the way.

As a minor note, to label the animals as "innocent" is inappropriate. Animals are not spirit creatures, for they have no capacity to form a relationship with God or to rebel against His authority. The words "innocent" and "guilty" apply no more to them than to my desk. Again we see the human tendency to anthropomorphize. We know that life cannot exist without death in the present order of nature, and God has a reason for this order.

A practical approach to refuting the claimed connection between old-earth beliefs and immorality is through personal testimony. Though I'm sure someone could name old-earth creationists who fail to teach and practice high moral standards (as could be done with any group of human beings, including young-earth creationists), I can name many who have taught and fought earnestly for biblical faith and godly living. Dr. David Rogstad is one. A physicist at the Caltech Jet Propulsion Laboratory, Dave is a devoted family man, has led many friends and strangers to Christ, led Bible studies, assisted in planting a church in his community, presented the gospel overseas as a short-term missionary, and has preached tirelessly in favor of morality and godliness. His wife and children, friends, and coworkers do not hesitate to honor him for his Christlike character.

Severing the False Link to Apostasy

I could name many others besides Dave Rogstad—pastors and ministry leaders, seminary professors, homemakers, businesspeople, truck drivers, teachers, nurses, accountants, attorneys, etc.—people from all backgrounds and all walks of life who remain unswervingly devoted to Christ, respecting His Word and walking in His ways, who believe that God created over long time spans.

Personal encounters with these obviously sincere Christians seem to have greater impact on young-universe creationists than does any amount of scientific evidence. Most young-earthers I know who have changed their view to old earth have done so after becoming convinced that old-earth creationists really do love the Lord and His Word and look forward to His return. I have observed this phenomenon many times, firsthand.

One young man who came to a class I taught on Revelation was profoundly shocked to discover I take biblical end-times prophecies literally. He was amazed to learn I had been an evangelism pastor. When he began to hear personal stories from class members about conversions to Christ resulting from that ministry, he finally relinquished belief in the equation that old-earth creationism = no soul-winning or spiritual growth.

One reason such myths about old-earth creationists have long and widely held sway is old-universe proponents' lack of prominence and outspokenness. These obstacles will be difficult to overcome. Most old-earthers I know are reserved. Many could be described as shy and introverted. These adjectives apply especially to the scientists among them. They are not lacking for courage in their personal witness, but they rarely picture themselves as champions of a public campaign or of public debate. Nor do they have wealthy backers promoting them. They typically use a one-to-one approach in pointing the world toward Christ.

What gives me hope for change, for dispelling the myths and misconceptions surrounding acceptance of a scientifically credible creation time scale, is seeing the flexibility and alertness of many evangelical congregations around the country. I see a willingness, especially recently, to consider the needs, interests, and barriers of the community around them and to adapt their ministries accordingly without compromise. Rigidity, dogmatism, suspicion, and certain traditions are being recognized as counterproductive. In an atmosphere of relaxed confidence, where dialogue is open, welcome, and nonthreatening, we can more effectively than ever fulfill God's purposes for His people.

CHAPTER NINE

Scientific Evidences for the Universe's Age

While the biblical and theological evidences certainly do permit and in some cases even imply a creation time scale far greater than the few thousand years of Ussher's chronology, the scientific evidences explicitly and overwhelmingly affirm it. Hundreds of reliable scientific tools demonstrate that the creation (all but modern man) is *old*. In perhaps the most amazing scientific breakthrough of the century, we have gained the capacity to measure the size and age of the cosmos. Science has given our generation what no other generation has had the privilege to see: a portrait depicting in remarkable detail the physical event, the creation miracle, recorded in Genesis 1:1. The portrait goes further, too, in supporting and amplifying the creation chronology, but for now let's focus on that initial wonder.

Three Simple Methods

Given today's technology, the universe of stars and galaxies is a much simpler system to measure and interpret than anyone but an astronomer might imagine. The dynamics of stars and galaxies can be understood and accurately predicted by applying only the laws of gravitational motion. To make matters easier, stars are so distant from each other they can be treated mathematically as points, rather than as complex systems. Furthermore, the motions of stars and galaxies take place in the near perfect vacuum of outer space, and virtually all the stars are comprised of gases (hydrogen and helium for the most part) right through to their core.

For all these reasons, straightforward physics — gas laws, thermodynamics, gravity, and nuclear physics — can give us secure estimates of the ages of stars, of galaxies, and of the cosmos itself. And I believe the non-scientist can understand how scientists arrive at these estimates.

The three easiest to understand methods for age-dating the universe involve the expansion of the universe, the burning of stars, and the abundances of radioactive elements.

1. *Expansion of the universe.* Astronomers have been able to measure the motion and speed of galaxies and the even older, more power-packed bodies called quasars. What they see is that the farther away the object, the faster it is moving away. This set of facts tells us that the universe is expanding outward from a starting point in space and time.

In a universe that expands outward from an infinitesimally small volume, the distances between the galaxies result from the velocity of expansion multiplied by the time of the expansion. So with a measure of the distances to the galaxies and the velocity of expansion (correcting for the expected slight slowdown of expansion that results from the gravitational pull of the galaxies on one another) we can calculate how long the universe has been expanding (time = distance/velocity). That is, we can figure out how old the universe is in the same way we could calculate when a grenade was detonated, given measurements of the distances between the still-moving grenade fragments and the rate of the exploding grenade's expansion.

The more measurements we have for the velocities and distances of galaxies and quasars, especially for those farthest away from us, the more accurate our calculation will be. The latest efforts by astronomers have produced results accurate to about 15 percent.[1-3]

Confirmation of this expansion-time measurement comes from observations of both the temperature and the smoothness of the background radiation left over from the initial explosive event in which the universe came to be. (We know the universe must have arisen from an extremely hot, extremely compact explosive creation event since only such an event could possibly yield the enormous amount of entropy the universe is observed to possess.[4])

An analogy for these kinds of observations would be using an array of thermometers placed at a certain distance from the open door of a once hot oven. At a certain distance from the oven's door, measuring the temperature of the air and the temperature differences from one thermometer to the next would tell us how long ago the oven door was opened.

Suppose the oven were surrounded by thousands of thermometers, each placed exactly ten feet from the center of the oven cavity. Suppose also that some time after the oven had been heated, turned off, and its door opened, each thermometer indicated exactly the same temperature. The only reasonable conclusion would be that the heat flow from the oven cavity to the room totally dominated the normal, temperature-disturbing air flows in the room. Such dominance would imply that the original temperature of the oven cavity must have been much greater than the room's temperature. And if all those thousands of thermometers indicated a very low temperature, we would conclude that considerable time had passed since the opening of the oven door.

Keep this oven picture in mind in considering how astronomers have been able to make conclusions about the age of the universe. They have simply measured the temperature and the smoothness of the temperature of the radiation left over throughout the cosmos from that initial hot burst with which the cosmos began. The result is a measure of the age of the universe entirely consistent with the age calculated from the velocities and distances of galaxies and quasars.

2. *Stellar burning.* Like flames from a burning log, the color and brightness of a star's flames tell us how long the star has been burning (provided we know the star's mass).

But we can come up with a much more accurate measure for the star than we can for a log. The star's composition (essentially hydrogen and helium) is much simpler than the log's; external effects are negligible (the external environment is basically a vacuum); the star is all gas; and the burning mechanism, nuclear fusion, is well understood and experimentally confirmed. In fact, stellar burning is simple enough to make it the most accurate indicator of the universe's age.

Astronomers have observed the colors and measured the brightnesses of millions of stars. Through these measurements they have found the range of ages for stars from the youngest to the oldest. With straightforward determinations of how long the universe must have been expanding before stars could form, astronomers simply add the age of the oldest stars to the time necessary for star formation to begin (about 1.5 billion years) to discover the age of the universe.

The lastest age estimates based on stellar burning have uncertainties of 10 to 15 percent.[5-7] However, once a few calibration problems are sorted out (potentially within 1994), that estimate should be precise to within about 5 percent.[8]

3. *Abundances of radioactive elements.* The only entity in the universe (outside nuclear physics laboratories) that can produce radioactive elements heavier than iron is supernovae. Only in supernovae are the energy densities sufficient.

Supernovae are super-giant stars in their final, powerfully explosive stages of burning. By applying classical mechanics (Newton's laws of motion) to the dynamics of galaxies, we find that a bunch of supernovae events must have occurred early in the history of the cosmos. But relatively few have occurred since. (Scientists have recently learned that life would not be possible apart from this pattern of events.[9])

Since radioactive decay proceeds according to well-understood, measurable physical processes, we can use the abundances (that is, the relative quantities) of various radioactive elements to estimate how much time has passed since these elements were produced in that burst of supernova activity. (Each supernova produces a fixed amount of radioactive elements.) We know the universe cannot be older than a certain age because some radioactive elements still exist. Uranium^{238} and thorium^{232}, for example, with radioactive half-lives of several billion years, can still be found. Therefore, we know that the universe cannot be as old as a trillion years, for if it were, all the uranium and thorium would have decayed into lighter elements.

On the other hand, the universe cannot be very young because most radioactive elements no longer exist at all. The radioactive elements with half-lives of millions of years or less (except the byproducts of other radioactive elements with longer half-lives and the products of local or cosmic radiation) are completely gone. Enough time has elapsed for every bit of these elements to decay away. Therefore, the universe and the earth must be at least a billion years old.

The amount of each radioactive element produced by the early supernovae can be precisely determined by measuring the identical processes in nuclear physics experiments. And, by comparing the relative elemental abundances of very distant supernovae with those of nearby supernovae, astronomers can confirm that the amounts of radioactive elements produced in past events are the same as in present events. By comparing how much of each radioactive element still exists with the amounts that must have been produced by the supernovae during that epoch when so many exploded, we can tell how much time has passed. As in the case of stellar burning, astrophysicists simply add that time to the time required for the first super-giant stars to form (approximately 1.5 billion years) to get a rough date for the beginning of the universe (about 17 billion years ago).

The Creationists' Response

What do young-universe creationists say about these age determinations? In my reading and discussions I have met the following five challenges, listed along with my replies:

Challenge 1: **Astronomers are wrong about the distances to stars and galaxies.**

Reply: The implication is that astronomers determine the distances of cosmic objects by only one method: the redshifts of spectral lines. And because redshift measurements of distances may possibly be off by a large percentage, the distances reported by astronomers are considered unreliable.

This, however, is not true. Astronomers use a wide variety of distance measuring tools. Whole textbooks have been devoted to these measuring methods. While disagreement does exist over which are the most reliable, the uncertainties hover around 10 to 15 percent, with very few as high as 50 percent, for the entire gamut of measurements and calibrations.[10] In other words, our measurements to the "edge" of the universe may be off by 15 percent, possibly a bit more, but certainly no more than 50 percent. Thus, suggesting that astronomers are in error by 100 percent is without support.

Here is another consideration: If the stars are really near rather than distant, they must be extremely tiny, far tinier than the minimum size necessary for a star to burn.[11] And if stars are neither distant nor tiny, another problem arises: Such massive luminous objects so close would light up the night sky as bright as day. There would never be darkness on Earth.

Challenge 2: **God could have created the light waves already in transit.**

Reply: Some young-universe creationists concede that the stars and galaxies really are as distant as astronomers claim. What they suggest to escape the connection between size and age is that the light waves from stars and galaxies did not come to us from the stars and galaxies but were created already spanning the distance or were set in motion from points partway between their sources and earth. This argument obviously belongs to the appearance-of-age category. The overlooked fact here is that star light and galaxy light give direct indications of their travel distances. The spectral lines (light waves at various frequencies) of stars and galaxies are broadened in direct proportion to the distance they travel. The random motions of gas clouds in space cause this effect. The radiation between the spectral lines, called the continuum, grows redder as it travels through interstellar and intergalactic dust. This reddening, like the effect of forest fire smoke on our view of the sun, is directly proportional to the distance the light has traveled.

Both theory and observations confirm that the broadening and reddening effects are reliable indicators of light-travel time and distance, even up to billions of light years. If God sent the light of stars and galaxies from points only some 10,000 light years away (not from the objects themselves), we would see a broadening and reddening indicative of 10,000 light years. We do not. What we see indicates light-travel times as great as 14 or 15 billion years.

To suggest that God artificially fixed the broadening and reddening of the light individually from 10 billion-trillion stars and 100 billion galaxies is to say that He deliberately deceived us. Such action seems contradictory to His revealed character and purpose and His statements that the creation is a truthful witness.

Challenge 3: **Light may have traveled faster a few thousand years ago.**

Reply: The work of two Australian creationists has been widely publicized among proponents of a young universe. Barry Setterfield and Trevor Norman teamed up to propose that the reason the universe appears old is that light used to travel much faster than it does today.[12] Given decay in light's velocity, the present value of the velocity of light would yield an inaccurate measure of the size and age for the universe.

The basis for this claim is a misinterpretation of data from speed-of-light measurements made over many years. What the data actually show is the increasing refinement of measurements, not a change in velocity.

The first calculation of the speed of light was attempted in 1675 by Olaus Römer, a Danish astronomer. His figure was about 3 percent higher than the modern measurements show. But the uncertainty in his measurement exceeded 3 percent. Recently, three American physicists reworked Römer's calculations. They found that if Römer had had more precise data for one part of his calculation, his speed-of-light figure would have agreed with the modern measurements to within 0.5 percent.[13]

Apparently the article describing this research was misunderstood by the Australians. They took the 1675 speed figure as evidence for the speed of light decreasing by 0.5 percent since 1675.[14,15] Actually, more than fifty measurements of the velocity of light have been made since Römer's, and when the uncertainties for each of the measurements are taken into account, the velocity shows itself constant through the more than 300 years since ground-based measurements began.

Using other types of measurements, the speed of light proves constant over many more years. Studies on a particular spectral line of hydrogen from nearby galaxies shows its constancy over the last 18 million years. New measurements on that spectral line in very distant galaxies extend that confirmation to 14 billion years.[16,17]

Let me add a practical consideration. The existence of life in the universe requires the constancy of the speed of light. A significant change in the velocity of light would so radically disturb such things as the luminosities of the stars and the relative abundances of the elements as to ruin the possibility for life anywhere, anytime in the universe. Since the c in Einstein's equation, $E = mc^2$, stands for the speed of light, a change in that figure would necessarily mean changes in the m (matter) or E (energy) or both, an alteration contradicted by abundant observations. If Setterfield and Norman were right, either Adam and Eve would have been incinerated by the sun's heat or the elements essential for building their bodies would not exist. Calling Einstein's equation into question will not help Setterfield and Norman's case either. A recent experiment has confirmed the accuracy of Einstein's equation to at least twenty-one places of the decimal (within 0.0000000000000000001 percent!).[18]

Challenge 4: **Light may take a shortcut through space.**

Reply: This argument arises from the work of young-universe creationist Harold Slusher,[19] who picks up an idea proposed in 1953 by Parry Moon and Domina Spencer.[20] Moon and Spencer were trying to overthrow Einstein's theory of relativity. They suggested that while space is Euclidean (that is, relatively flat) for stars and galaxies, light on the other hand travels in highly curved Riemannian space. In their geometric system, light from the most distant galaxies would reach us in just sixteen years. Thus, Slusher points out, the light-travel times of the stars and galaxies would not conflict with a universe only thousands of years old.

What Slusher fails to acknowledge is that Moon and Spencer never produced the mathematics to support their assumptions.[21] Neither did they address numerous difficulties in their hypothesis. For one, their hypothesis implies that light would travel to us from the stars and galaxies in two different directions. This means that we would see duplicate images of all the stars and galaxies. Clearly, this is not what astronomers observe. Also, Moon and Spencer wrote their paper before overwhelming proof for Einstein's theory of relativity became available.[22]

Challenge 5: **Were you there?**

Reply: By this question young-universe creationists imply that since no one was present when God created the universe and transformed it into its present state, no one can have any factual basis for theories on the origin and development of the universe. Therefore astronomers' calculations and conclusions about the age of the universe are pure speculation.

Ken Ham of the ICR makes these statements:

There were no observers to these long ago events.[23]

No one was there to record these past events. . . . Scientists only have the present — they do not have the past.[24]

Actually, the case is exactly opposite to what Ham says. Astronomers have only the past — they do not have the present. They cannot record present events. But they can record all manner of past events. For instance, when astronomers observe the sun, they are recording the physics of God's creation as it was eight minutes ago, for that is how long it took the light of the sun to travel to the astronomers' telescopes. When astronomers observe the Crab Nebula, they are recording the physics of God's creation as it was two thousand years before the birth of Jesus, for the Crab Nebula is 4,000 light years distant. In observing the Andromeda Galaxy, astronomers are testing physics as it was two million years ago. In detecting the tiny ripples in the cosmic background radiation astronomers are measuring the state of the universe as it was just 300,000 years after the creation event, some 17 billion years ago.

Because of the time it takes for light to travel from the stars, galaxies, and other sources to the astronomers' telescopes, their telescopes operate like time machines into the past. Astronomers can literally measure the heavens to see what God did in the past. In answer to the question, "Were you there?" astronomers can reply, "Yes, we were. We can see what happened back then because the report of it is reaching us today. Have a look for yourself to see how the heavens declare the glory of God."

Clearly, young-universe creationists are going to extreme lengths in their attempts to deny the astronomical evidences against their creation dates. The nature of their responses perhaps testifies to the strength of the proofs against their position.

The Science Community's Reply

The results derived by the three age-determining methods discussed earlier in this chapter, along with a few others, appear in table 9.1. These measurements and calculations yield consistent figures for the age of the universe — about 17 billion years, give or take a billion or two. The consistency argues strongly for certainty.

Table 9.1: Measurements of the Age of the Universe

For more details on the listed methods see my book The Fingerprint of God, *second edition (Orange, California: Promise Publishing, 1991), pages 81-93.*

Measuring Method	Age (billions of years)
relaxation times of star clusters	more than 4
erosion on Mercury, Mars, and the moon	more than 4
star stream interactions in galaxies	more than 8
expansion of the universe	15.5 ± 4.0
color-luminosity fitting	18.0 ± 2.4
nucleochronology	17.0 ± 4.0
deuterium abundance and mass density	19.0 ± 5.0
anthropic principles	17.0 ± 7.0

mean age – 17 ± 3 billion years

In testimony sent to the Supreme Court on the certainty of this date relative to the dates promoted by young-universe creationists, Caltech physicist and Nobel Laureate Murray Gell-Mann said it would be easier to believe in a flat earth than to believe the universe is 6,000 years old, or anything other than about 15 billion years old.

In "Farewell to Newton, Einstein, Darwin . . . ," *Science 81,* Allen Hammond and Lynn Margulis expressed the following view:

Adoption of creationist [i.e., young-universe creationist] "theory" requires, at a minimum, the abandonment of essentially all of modern astronomy, much of modern physics, and most of the earth sciences. Much more than evolutionary biology is at stake.[25]

There are many different models of origins under the banner of old-universe creationism. All go against at least some of the tenets of evolutionary biology. But young-universe creationism challenges virtually all of science.

People of all cultures and times have looked at the heavens and felt awed by the enormity of space. But few have grasped the connection between vastness and age. Perhaps that is why so many have been willing to believe that the universe is a few thousand rather than a few billion years old despite the abundant evidence.

I'm troubled to think what may happen when the connection between size and age becomes more widely known and understood. Many seekers and nonbelievers, if taught that a young universe is the unquestionable teaching of the Bible, will conclude, under the barrage of compelling scientific evidence for the antiquity of the universe, that the Bible must be false and thus turn away from considering the claims of Christ. Meanwhile many sincere Christians, trained in the tenets of young-universe creationism, will be thrown into consternation, falsely convinced that they must shut out science and its facts altogether to preserve their faith. How can we love the Lord our God with all our heart, soul, mind, and strength if we must separate our minds from our faith? Such a separation violates the very meaning of faith.

CHAPTER TEN

Is There Scientific Evidence for a Young Universe?

Most creationists with some science training who hold to a twenty-four-hour creation day insist that the evidences for a billions-of-years-old universe and earth are inconclusive. They argue that a considerable body of scientific material supports a young age. Walter Brown, Henry Morris, and Edward Blick claim anywhere from fifty to eighty separate scientific evidences for a universe and earth only thousands of years old.[1-3]

In this claim of scientific support for their beliefs, these young-universe creationists convince many whose science education and biblical training are insufficient to evaluate the evidence. All eighty of these "evidences" of a young age, when investigated closely, involve one or more of these four problems:

- Faulty assumptions
- Faulty data
- Misapplication of principles, laws, and equations
- Failure to consider opposing evidence

Ironically, these fallacious arguments, when corrected, provide some of the strongest evidences available for an old universe and an ancient earth. Ten such arguments that young-universe creationists use most often and presumably consider their strongest are listed here, along with replies.

Sample Evidence A: **The continents are eroding too quickly.** Erosion measurements show that the continents are lowered by wind, rain, etc., at a rate of about 0.05 millimeters per year. At this rate, the continents (averaging about 800 meters in elevation) would disappear in about 16 million years. Since continents do still have considerable elevation, the earth must be younger than 16 million years.

   Reply: This argument looks at one side of the equation only. The fallacy lies in its failure to acknowledge that lava flows, delta and continental shelf buildup (from eroded material), coral reef buildup, and uplift from colliding tectonic plates occur at rates roughly equivalent to, and in many cases far exceeding, the erosion rate. The Himalayas, for example, as a result of tectonic uplift, are rising at a rate of about 15 millimeters per year. The San Gabriel Mountains, just north of Los Angeles, are rising at an average rate of 9 millimeters per year. Lava flows have increased the land area of the state of Hawaii by several square miles since its admission into the United States in 1959.

   The scientific record agrees with Genesis 1:2,9-10 in stating that shortly after the earth's formation the planet's surface was more fully covered with water than at present.[4] Through the agency of volcanic eruptions, plate tectonic collisions, and other continent-building activities, the surface of Earth has progressed from 100 percent oceans and 0 percent continents to about 70 percent oceans and 30 percent continents. The reason continental land area is not increasing today is that the continents are being eroded down at roughly the same rate volcanos, plate tectonics, etc., are building them up.

   The amount of continental land mass added every year as a result of volcanos and tectonics is roughly independent of the total continental land area. But the amount of land mass eroded away is strongly dependent on the total continental land area. Therefore continental land area continues to increase until there is enough land area that the rate of erosion equals the rate of build up. The time required for the continents to build up from 0 percent of the global surface area to the present 30 percent (and equilibrium) takes about 2 billion years. Thus continental erosion is an argument for an old rather than a young earth.

Sample Evidence B: **Dust accumulates too quickly on the moon's surface.**

In the 1950s, before satellites were available to take direct measurements, geophysicist Hans Pettersson estimated the influx to Earth of material from meteors by measuring the quantity of nickel in the material passing through dust filters on top of Hawaii's Mount Mauna Loa.[5] Since nickel is much rarer in terrestrial dust than in meteorites, he assumed that all the nickel came from space. Knowing that meteoritic material is composed of 2.5 percent nickel, he used the amount of nickel collected to calculate that some 14 million tons of space dust settles on the earth every year. Applied to a 4-billion-year-old moon, this would add up to 145 feet of space dust on the moon. Since we now know of only about two-and-half inches of surface dust on the moon, this would imply an age for the moon not of billions of years but only of millions of years — 6 million to be exact. Pettersson warned of possible large errors and questionable assumptions, and these were used by young-universe creationists to whittle the 6 million years down to about 10,000 years.[6-8]

Reply: This argument draws on old, crude, contaminated estimates and ignores subsequent precise, pure measurements. As Pettersson himself was aware, his ground-based instrument was measuring not only dust infalling from outer space but also material thrown into the atmosphere by wind erosion and volcanic eruptions. Fortunately, about a decade after Pettersson's estimates were published, direct measurements by satellites of cosmic dust inflow were available. Instead of a 14-million-ton annual accumulation on the earth, only 23 thousand tons were indicated (11 thousand tons per year for the moon).[9] This quantity would translate into 1.2 inches of dust for a moon 4.5 billion years old. When other sources of inflow and outflow are accounted for (decomposition from ultraviolet radiation, other sources of erosion, inflow from larger meteorites and comets, and outflow from asteroid and meteorite impacts large enough to expel debris away from the reach of the moon's gravity), the measured 2.5 inches of lunar dust adds up to an age for the lunar surface of 4.25 billion years (a value in agreement with several other measurements of the moon's age).

Sample Evidence C: **The earth's magnetic field is decaying too rapidly.**
The earth's magnetic field has decreased steadily since measurements were first taken some 150 years ago. Based on the field strength of a typical magnetic star (certainly exceeding any conceivable value for Earth) and on the observed rate of decay, some creationists have calculated that the decay process must have begun on Earth no more than 10,000 years ago. Thus the earth's age must be 10,000 years or less.

   Reply: The problem with this evidence is that Earth's magnetic field does not undergo steady decay but rather follows a "sinusoidal" pattern. That is, the field decays, builds up, decays, builds up, etc. The proof for this pattern lies in ancient geologic strata found throughout the world. The rocks reveal that the earth's field reverses its polarity roughly every half million years. Each reversal process lasts roughly 10,000 years.[10]

Sample Evidence D: **The sun burns by gravitational contraction and thus must be young.**
Before the discovery of nuclear energy, the only explanation astronomers could offer for the enormous energy output of the sun and other stars was gravitational contraction. Given the diameter and energy output of our sun, we can calculate

that its maximum age would be about 100 million years *if* it were generating energy only by this process. When some measurements indicated a very slight decrease in the sun's diameter, a number of young-earth creationists concluded that the sun's energy output must arise only from the gravitational collapse of the sun, rather than from nuclear fusion processes at its core. Therefore, they surmised that the sun's age must be less than 100 million years.

Reply: Again, the argument overlooks significant data. First, it has been shown that if a body of our sun's dimensions were experiencing gravitational contraction, the temperature, pressure, and other conditions at its center would inevitably ignite nuclear fusion. Furthermore, various measured characteristics of the sun—including its effective temperature, luminosity, spectra, radius, outflow of neutrinos, and mass—all guarantee that the sun is burning by nuclear fusion and that this fusion has been proceeding for about 5 billion years. Additional experimental proof for this conclusion comes from several dozen exploded hydrogen bombs and the results from hundreds of experiments performed in the world's plasma physics laboratories.

As for the observed decrease in the sun's diameter, the measurements cited were later found to be at odds with other visual (i.e., naked eye) measurements. The conflict has since been laid to rest by the precise photoelectric measurements of Barry LaBonte and Robert Howard.[11] Their measurements show that during the period 1974 to 1981 the solar radius remained constant to within one part in 9,000.

Sample Evidence E: Galaxy clusters are not dispersed widely.

For a cluster of heavenly bodies to remain together (contained), the gravity of the system must be sufficient to overcome the velocities of the individual bodies within it. Armed with measurements of the velocities and masses for all the galaxies in a galaxy cluster, astronomers can calculate: (a) the dispersal time (time it takes for all the galaxies to leave the cluster) for clusters with total mass too small for gravitational containment; or (b) the relaxation time (time required for the galaxies to assume randomized velocities) for clusters with total mass large enough for containment. Some creationists point out that when such calculations are applied to galaxy clusters, the lack of observed galaxy dispersal indicates an age for the clusters much less than a billion years.

Reply: The problem with evidence E is that these calculations for dispersal and relaxation times assume not only that all the mass within the galaxy clusters is luminous but also that galaxies approximate point sources (those with diameters very much smaller than the average distances between them). On the contrary, sound evidence exists to conclude that most of the mass is non-luminous (that is, not shining by its own light production). And galaxies cannot be treated as point sources. In fact, their diameters are only about an order of magnitude smaller (that is, about ten times smaller) than the average distances between them within a given cluster. Therefore, calculations of the dispersal times for galaxy clusters are virtually meaningless.

By comparison, however, essentially all of the mass within star clusters is visible, and the stars within the clusters *are* point sources. The average distances between them are at least seven orders of magnitude greater (that is, about 10 million times greater) than their average diameters. When dispersal and relaxation time calculations are applied to star clusters in our galaxy, many clusters show their ages to be greater than 2 billion years.

Sample Evidence F: Granite crystal halos can arise from ^{218}Po decay only if the earth is young.

Polonium 218 is a radioactive isotope with a half-life of only three minutes. (Half-life is the time required for the radioactive decay of half the atoms in a sample of a radioactive isotope of an element.) Yet halos in granite crystals that appear to arise from the decay of polonium 218 show up in what seem to be basement or primordial rock deposits. If the halos arise from primordial polonium, then how did the surrounding rocks crystalize so rapidly that the crystals were ready to receive halo impressions from the decay of polonium?

The answer, according to young-earth creationist Robert Gentry, among others, is that geologists are wrong about their understanding of the processes shaping the earth shortly after its formation.[12] Instead, they say, God must have imposed the geological structures instantaneously. Therefore, measurements by geologists do not prove that the earth is old, nor can they be used to argue against a young earth.

Reply: Evidence F sounds impressive because it is so technical. Most people, even some scientists, are ill-equipped to evaluate its validity. My research into the matter indicates that there is no proof of halos in basement or primordial rocks, and likewise no evidence that halos arise *only* from the decay of polonium 218.

In his writings, Gentry is vague about the locations from which he obtained his granite crystal samples. Geologist Jeffrey Richard Wakefield actually visited all of Gentry's sample sites. Through a series of phone conversations with Gentry as well as a trip with him to one site, Wakefield pinpointed the exact locations from which all of Gentry's samples were taken. Wakefield discovered that in every case Gentry's samples came not from primordial granites as he had claimed, but rather from young dikes (igneous rock infusions into vertical fissures) that crosscut older igneous and sedimentary rocks.[13,14]

Two more geologists, Leroy Odom and William Rink, recently published an independent response to Gentry's polonium-decay hypothesis.[15] They began by pointing out that there are three classes of unexplained radio halos. In the case of one class, the giant halos, Odom and Rink explained them by another geological process called hole diffusion. (I hesitate to bring it up because it, too, is far too complicated to explain in a few words to those who are not geologists or solid-state physicists. I would ask you to confirm this research with other geologists and solid-state physicists.) Growth of halos by hole diffusion is an ultraslow process that would argue for an old earth rather than for instantaneous creation. The authors infer that since one of the three "mysterious" classes of radio halos has now been explained in terms of normal (old-earth), known physical processes, it is reasonable to conclude that the same will eventually be accomplished for the two remaining classes, including Gentry's polonium 218 halos. In their summary they state that Gentry's data "requires neither unknown radioactivity nor an abandonment of current concepts of geologic time."[16]

Sample Evidence G: **Rapid sedimentation and peat deposition following the 1980 Mount Saint Helens eruption demonstrate that all geological processes are not gradual, but rapid.**

Within a relatively brief period of time (a few months to a few years) following the violent eruption of Mount Saint Helens, peat layers (the first stage in the formation of coal) and sedimentary rock already had formed in the vicinity of the volcano. This phenomenon seemed to young-earth creationists to challege the notion that geologic layers are deposited according to gradual uniformitarian processes taking place over millions and hundreds of millions of years.[17] They concluded that geological processes provide evidences for a young earth and not for an old earth.

Reply: The problem lies in the assumption that *all* geological processes either take place gradually at relatively uniform (i.e., constant) rates or rapidly at rates pulsed by major catastrophes. The young-earth versus old-earth debate is pictured in this context as a battle between the principles of uniformitarianism and the principles of catastrophism, with one significant twist. Catastrophism as defined by geologists refers to the formation of geologic structures through a variety of catastrophes occurring at different times. Young-earth creationists define catastrophism as the formation of *all*

Earth's major geologic structures by a single catastrophic event, namely the Genesis flood, occurring during a ten-and-a-half-month period five to fifteen thousand years ago.

This use of the Mount Saint Helens data exemplifies the "either-or" fallacy (that is, it sets up an unfounded dilemma). Geology reflects the operation of both slow and rapid processes. As geophysics textbooks explain, some geological features can be explained *only* by gradual processes occurring at relatively fixed rates over many millions of years.[18,19] Examples would be coral atolls, varves, anthracite coal, and certain conglomerate and metamorphic layers.

In the case of coral atolls, scientists can measure the daily accumulation of band-like deposits over millions of years. From these deposits they can make many determinations, including the rate of slowing of the earth's rotation period. Such deposits establish that the earth's rotation period has been slowing down at *exactly* the same rate over the last 400 million years.[20,21] Coral atolls serve as one example of the principle of uniformitarianism and as evidence that the earth is hundreds of millions of years old.

Other geological formations can be explained *only* by rapid processes occurring in punctuated pulses. Examples include lava flows, avalanche scars, asteroid and meteorite craters, polar ice cap shifts, and intrusions. For each of these examples an abundance of evidence exists for repeated disasters over the last few billion years. Astronomers can calculate, for example, the rate of asteroid and meteorite impacts and compare their calculations with the numbers of craters and the degree of weathering at the existing crater sites both here on Earth and on Mercury, Venus, the moon, Mars, and the moons of Jupiter and Saturn. The numbers and the observed weathering show that the craters did not occur at one time by one catastrophe but rather by many catastrophes stretched over the last few billion years.

Many more geological formations are clearly a combination of both gradual and rapid processes. The Grand Canyon, for example, reveals intrusions penetrating through several sedimentary layers.

Evidence of rapid geological processes, like those witnessed as a result of the 1980 Mount Saint Helens eruption, do not prove that every structure in the crust of the earth occurred quickly. They simply illustrate that geology is a complex science revealing both gradual and rapid processes at work over the entire history of the earth's crust.

Sample Evidence H: **Since computer models of the spiral structure of galaxies show that the spiral collapses after two or three rotations, spiral galaxies must be much younger than astronomers claim.**

Isaac Newton's laws of motion enable us to calculate with considerable precision the dynamics of large rotating systems of points, or stars. (Stars are radiant "points" to observers on the earth. The distances between them are so much greater than their diameters that by comparison they are points.) When Kevin Prendergast made such calculations twenty-five years ago, he discovered that a large system of stars will establish a spiral structure only in a few rotations and that after two or three more rotations the structure will collapse into a sphere or an ellipsoid. Since we know that galaxies take only a few hundred million years to rotate, the existence of a significant number of spiral galaxies in the universe today, according to certain young-universe creationists, proves they cannot be as old as the 9 to15 billion years that astronomers claim. Instead, they must be less than 2 billion years old.[22] If they are less than 2 billion years old, then astronomers cannot be trusted in their age calculations, and perhaps the universe is only thousands of years old.

Reply: The argument based on evidence H overlooks the continuing research by Prendergast and others. In the years following his initial computer modeling efforts, Prendergast discovered that ongoing star formation stabilizes the spiral structure.[23] Specifically, he demonstrated that as long as new stars continue to form at a significant rate within a galaxy, the spiral structure will be maintained. But as soon as star formation ceases, the spiral structure will collapse within the next two or three rotations.

Prendergast's discovery beautifully dovetails with astronomers' observations of galaxies. In spherical and ellipsoidal galaxies, astronomers see no evidence of ongoing star formation, whereas in the spiral galaxies such evidence is abundant. And, the farther away astronomers look (that is, the farther back in time they see), the more spiral galaxies they observe.

In the vicinity of our galaxy only 6 percent of the galaxies are spirals; at a distance of some 4 billion light years (4 billion years ago), 30 percent of all the galaxies are spirals; and at 10-billion-light-years distance (10 billion years ago), about half of all the galaxies are spirals.[24,25] This pattern is exactly what astronomers would expect in a universe some 15 to 18 billion years old. According to their models, the galaxies would form at approximately the same time, and as the galaxies age, more and more of their gas and dust condenses into stars. Eventually all of the gas and dust is consumed and star formation ceases, bringing about the collapse of the spiral structures. Thus, as the universe gets older, fewer galaxies will remain as spirals.

Since spiral galaxies still exist, the universe cannot be any older than about 25 billion years. Because only 6 percent of the galaxies near our own are spirals, the universe cannot be any younger than about 12 billion years.

A corroboration of this conclusion comes from Prendergast's modeling of collisions and close encounters among galaxies.[26] As mentioned in a previous chapter, galaxies are relatively close together. Consequently, astronomers have the opportunity to see many galaxy collisions and close encounters in progress. Using data on the velocity and position of galaxies, they can calculate the rate of collisions and close encounters for any particular galaxy. In modeling the dynamics of two or more galaxies closely passing one another, Prendergast was able to determine in what ways the spiral arms of galaxies are distorted by close encounters and collisions. Looking for such distortions in spiral galaxies close to our own, Prendergast was able to calculate from their number and type just how long such galaxies have existed. The answer is consistent with the number of spiral galaxies and with the observations of star formation—galaxies have existed for 10 to 15 billion years. Thus, in every way, the spiral structure of galaxies argues for a universe billions of years old rather than thousands of years.

Sample Evidence I: **Trails of "human" footprints alongside, and sometimes crossing over, trails of dinosaur prints prove that dinosaurs were contemporary with humans.**
The observation of a few footprints that appear to be human prints alongside a great many prints that were clearly made by dinosaurs has been interpreted by many young-earth creationists as proof that dinosaurs and men lived together.[27-29] This fact would imply that dinosaurs were thriving as recently as a few thousand years ago. It would also imply that the geological strata in which the prints were found could not have been deposited tens of millions of years ago but only in the last few thousand years. Therefore the dinosaurs and the strata of the earth are not relics from an ancient past but have existed only for about ten thousand years.

Reply: The first assumption that must be addressed is that prints in close proximity necessarily establish contemporaneous existence. This assumption is false. The earth's strata can be disturbed and redisturbed by events occurring at different times, especially in a river bed like that at Glen Rose, Texas, where most of the "human" footprints have been found. But this faulty assumption is not the main defect of the argument from evidence I. The more serious problem lies in the identification of the prints as human.

The dinosaur prints at the sites in question belong to tridactyls, three-toed carnivorous dinosaurs. The viscosity and composition of the mud, the weight of the subject, the way they walked, and the degree of erosion determine how perfectly formed and preserved prints will be. These factors affect the prints not only of dinosaurs but also of all other creatures. If I were to walk barefoot through a patch of mud, the depth, composition, and viscosity of that mud would determine how distinct the impressions from my feet would be. If the depth or other factors were varied, some of my prints would be much more sharply defined than others. Similarly, given variations in the mud, the dinosaur prints in question are small and unclear enough to resemble human footprints.

Indications that the "human" footprints were made by dinosaurs comes from these additional observations:

- The footprints are too far apart to have been made by humans. They fit well, however, the stride of the dinosaurs.
- Most of the "human" prints are too large to have been made by humans.
- Many of the "human" prints show dinosaur features, for example, claw marks, anterior V-shaped splaying, fissure patterns, and drag or swish marks from a tail or snout.
- Almost all of the prints have indentations and colorations uniquely indicative of tridactyl dinosaurs.
- The "human" prints often form a line that continues as a path of near-perfect tridactyl footprints.
- Prints that were claimed to be "human" turn out to be mere erosion patterns in the strata.

For these reasons and others, both secular and Christian scholars have concluded there is no factual basis for claiming that any of the footprints in question are human.[30-33] To their credit, some young-earth creationists have ceased from using this argument and removed books and films about it from circulation.[34-35]

Sample Evidence J: **Since a comet's average lifespan is only a couple of thousand years, given the rather limited supply**

of comets, their present existence proves the solar system cannot be any older than a few thousand years.

Comets orbiting the solar sytem, such as Halley's comet, are reported to disintegrate in about two thousand years on the average. Every time a comet swings close by the sun, the heat and light of the sun boil away a significant portion of the comet's mass. After a few dozen revolutions, none of the comet remains. Since comets are observed orbiting the sun, the solar system must be only a few thousand years old.[36]

Reply: Estimates cited in evidence J for the average lifespan of comets date back to the 1970s. At that time no space-based measurements of comets were available, and what data did exist was weighted heavily by easy-to-see comets. The easiest comets to see are those that pass closest to the sun, and these comets suffer the most rapid disintegration. Hence, estimates previous to 1980 of the average lifespans for comets have since proven to be far too low.

In 1986 five spacecraft visited Halley's comet and made the first accurate measurements of both its mass and its rate of disintegration. Astronomers determined that Halley's comet is massive enough to survive at least another 500 revolutions around the sun.[37] With observations of Halley's comet going back to 240 BC, and knowing that it passes the sun every seventy-six years, we can calculate the approximate minimum lifespan for this comet at 40,000+ years.

Halley's comet is unusual in that it has such a short period of revolution. Much more typical are comets such as Kohoutek, which comes around the sun every 80,000 years, or Pons-Brooks and Griggs-Mellish, every 3,000,000 years. Five hundred revolutions for these comets would yield lifespans of 40 million and 1.5 billion years respectively.

But most comets do not revolve around the sun or any other star. Astronomers observe them passing by the sun along parabolic or hyperbolic paths. Objects traveling along such paths will never return. Technically, these comets are not members of our solar sytem. Like the sun, they orbit the center of the galaxy and like the sun, they are repeatedly jostled by the gravitational tugs of stars in their vicinity. Occasionally, such tugs will send them on a near encounter with the sun. If they come close enough to the sun, they will heat up sufficiently to become visible to astronomers. But such occurrences are rare. The great majority never get close enough for astronomers to detect them easily. Given the number of comets that astronomers do see, the population of comets in interstellar space must exceed the trillions.

Comets are not about to disappear. They are made up of dust, rocks, and frozen gases, debris left over from star formation. They may, like the stars, continue to condense from the huge gas and dust clouds abundant near the sun's orbital path around the center of our galaxy. Given the supply of gas and dust measured to exist around the spiral arms of our galaxy and the huge number of stars that have recently formed in our galaxy, astronomers could look forward to observing comets of all types for another 10 billion years, if the earth were to last that long. (Scientifically it can't because the sun can last only another 6 billion years. I believe it won't because God has promised to replace the entire universe with new heavens as soon as the problem of evil is conquered, and the Bible suggests that that time is not far off.)

Even the supply of comets with short orbital periods is not at all threatened. A small percentage of the long-period comets and comets traveling along parabolic and hyperbolic paths will get tugged enough by the gravitational pulls of the planets for their paths to transform from very large ellipses, hyperbolas, and parabolas into small, elliptical orbits about the sun. Multiplying this small percentage by the total number of comets that could be so perturbed yields a number big enough to explain *all* the short-period comets, both those that are presently observed and those that existed in the past 5-billion-year history of our solar system.

———

Other scientific evidences and arguments for a young universe or for a young earth similarly can be demonstrated to be fallacious. Some young-universe creationists with whom I've discussed the fallacious nature of their evidences have admitted privately to me that they really have no solid scientific evidence for their belief. Others, like physicist Gerald Aardsma of the Institute for Creation Research, in essence write off the need for independent scientific support, saying, "I don't care whether the whole scientific community thinks I'm a fool."[39]

Talk radio host John Stewart asked John Morris (a geological engineer) in my presence if he or any of his associates had ever met or heard of a scientist who became convinced that the earth or universe is only thousands of years old based on scientific evidence, without any reference to a particular interpretation of the Bible. Morris answered honestly, "No."[40] Stewart has since asked the same question of several other prominent young-universe proponents, and the answer has been consistent: *no*.[41]

The vigor with which young-universe creationists proclaim scientific support, knowing that it does not exist outside their own circle, leads some secularists to impugn their motives. Secular scientists have made very nasty, condemning remarks in print and broadcast media. The statements by Gell-Mann, Hammond, and Margulis are tame in comparison with some I have heard (see chapter 9, pages 91-102).

These accusers fail to consider the background. From the young-earth creationists' perspective, the line that was drawn in the sand a couple of centuries ago—the line between faith in biblical truth and faith in scientific fact—has not moved. Driven largely by the fear of biological naturalistic evolution, the line for many still rests on the issue of age—the age of the universe, the age of the earth, the age of life and death. Most have been raised with this false, "either-or" dilemma, and they are compelled to deny physical reality to keep their faith. I'm saddened to think of what living with this tension must be like, especially as I recall the old adage, "The heart cannot rejoice in what the mind rejects."

CHAPTER ELEVEN

Acceptance
of Physical Reality

Christians' struggle over the time-scale issue is not the first needless "battle for faith." Whenever new discoveries cause a shift in some people's view of the world (or cosmos), the change meets with resistance while those people, including Christians, consider the view's effect on long-held beliefs. When the view touches on what are considered non-negotiable doctrines and principles, there is good reason for caution and careful rethinking. History shows that some adjust too readily through careless compromise. Others refuse to adjust at all, championing the resistance and, whether wisely or foolishly, sometimes becoming martyrs in the process.

Galileo and Geocentrism

Perhaps the most famous example in Christendom of resistance to new truth was the church's reaction to Galileo. Many have read or heard the story of the Roman Catholic prelates who refused to look through his telescope. If they had, they would have seen for themselves the phases and motions of the solar system planets and moons. So fearful were they to see a sun-centered system of planets, believing it contradicted Scripture and weakened the authority of the church, that they preferred to look the other way. And they were not subtle about their adherence to illusions. Cardinal Bellarmine formally admonished Galileo for advocating what he called "realist Copernicanism."[1]

Parents of the Healed Blind Man

Examples of resistance to reality may be seen in times long before ours and Galileo's. One of the earliest recorded examples is found in John 9. The Pharisees questioned the parents of the man who was healed by Jesus Christ from congenital blindness.

Unwilling to acknowledge either the healing or the Healer, the parents would confirm only that the man was their son and that he was born blind. Their reason for avoiding the obvious becomes clear in verse 22: fear. They feared the multiple repercussions of accepting the reality of Jesus' power to heal; in particular they feared being put out of the synagogue, cut off from the heart of their social life and cultural identity. No wonder they struggled.

Early Anti-Physical Sects

One of the gravest problems in the fledgling church of the first and second centuries was the emergence of sects that taught the material realm—i.e., all of nature—was utterly and irretrievably ruined and evil. Good, according to these groups, resided only in the spiritual domain, never in the physical.

Members of such sects denied their own physical being, postulating that the physical part of themselves and of the universe around them was unreal. The evidence from their five senses meant nothing since material entities were imaginary or illusory. In this view, individuals needn't be held accountable for their treatment of the physical world or for their physical actions within it. Nor did they ever need to come to grips with an all-loving, all-powerful God who allowed humans to experience pain and suffering. According to these sects, pain and suffering belonged to the physical realm, which was not real.

Another belief held in common by these early anti-physical sects was that people could be divided into three or more distinct spiritual strata. At the top were the ones possessing privileged spiritual knowledge. Only individuals manifesting a prescribed spirituality (manifesting certain behaviors, etc.) could ever attain this level. A second class of people were those who had faith in God but fell short of qualification to attain "higher knowledge." The lowest class of humanity were those who clung to their material world views. They were subject to matter.

An elite few were thought to dwell in the top strata. A significantly larger number of people were said to occupy the second level. But the vast majority of the human race comprised the bottom level. Members of this majority were condemned irretrievably to destruction.

These anti-physical beliefs are appealing because much in our lives is physically, emotionally, and spiritually painful. The effects of sin, evil, suffering, and death are difficult to face. Integrating these harsh realities with a loving, omniscient, omnipotent God can be difficult. But, if these things are not real, then there is no need to be churned up over this problem. We can reinterpret painful events and feel smugly superior to those people who have not "graduated" to our level. Anti-physical beliefs provide a convenient antidote for treating the unwanted pains and insecurities of life.

Biblical Response to Anti-Physicalism

Despite the obvious appeal of these anti-physical sects, early Christians stood firmly against those teachings. Elitism blatantly contradicts the New Testament message of equality before God, all believers belonging to one body, all parts of the body being equally important to the whole (1 Corinthians 12:12-26, Galatians 3:26-29), and God's redemption extended to every person (John 3:16). Even before the New Testament became widely available among Christians, they took seriously the instructions of the Old, which calls God's people to face the realities of the physical world and to turn to God for help. The legitimate fears and temptations we humans share concerning sin, evil, suffering, and death are meant to turn us to God for mercy and compassion, not away from physical reality.

Anti-Physical Trends Today

Anti-physical beliefs have persisted through the centuries, sometimes spawning cults. These abound in the twentieth century. Through the work of the Christian Research Institute, Spiritual Counterfeits Project, and other organizations, these groups are identified and studied for the sake of effective ministry to their members and the protection of unwary truth seekers.

I believe there's a need for alertness within the camp of Christian orthodoxy to the encroachment of anti-physical notions. Few Christians are yet aware of the anti-physical tendency within young-universe creationism. Most creationists are unaware of it themselves. As an example, young-universe creationists deny the reality of the universe astronomers observe and measure. When astronomers demonstrate that the light from the Andromeda galaxy takes 2 million years to reach us, young-universe creationists claim "knowledge" that the universe is only about ten thousand years old. Astronomers must be wrong, because Andromeda cannot reside where researchers say it does (see pages 96-100). All the galaxies astronomers observe, nearly one trillion of them, must be scenes that God painted on the sky.

Even supernova explosions (eruptions that cause a single star to outshine 10 billion others), such as the one that occurred in the Large Magellanic Cloud in 1987, must be denied. Since that supernova measures some 80,000 light years away, and since young-universe creationists deny physical events prior to about 10,000 years ago, they are forced to conclude that we are not seeing what occurred 80,000 years ago. We are seeing, they suggest, a complete, detailed history of events that never happened.

Even events taking place in the present are denied. Many young-universe creationists claim that star formation is one of God's miracles of creation and, therefore, could take place only during the appropriate Genesis creation day.[2-7] Like the Roman Catholic clerics who refused to look through Galileo's telescope, they refuse to look for themselves at the various stages of star formation that can be observed daily in the cosmos.

I must be careful to add that most young-universe creationists do not actually refer to the stars and galaxies and events in the universe as "mirages," "nonexistent," or "not occurring." They prefer to use such terms as "illusions" or "apparent."

This denial of physical reality is not limited to reinterpreting astronomical bodies and phenomena. According to young-universe creationists, the fossils do not represent ancient creatures; nor are coal, oil, gas, and top soil the remains of thousands of previous generations of life; nor do the stratified layers of the earth's crust testify of rocks subjected to past pressures, erosions, and stresses; nor do tree rings, coral banding, and ice layers represent real years past; nor does the erosion of craters and mountains on the earth and on the planets and moons result from ongoing natural processes.

According to young-universe creationists, all these things must be illusions, and our "knowing" anything apart from the words of the Bible cannot be trusted. Consequently, virtually all of science must have led humankind astray. Secular scientists' research means little, for these people lack the special knowledge available only through the biblical filter — the "right" biblical filter. Evangelical or fundamentalist scientists who disagree with the young-universe creationists' view can be ignored or discredited, for those who disagree have succumbed to "interpreting the Bible through the eyeglasses of science." They have rejected the "biblical knowledge" that could set them straight and turn them from leading themselves and others into apostasy. Some young-earth creationists see themselves as having a corner on truth about the cosmos.

Ironically, while young-universe creationists often and sometimes loudly demand equal access in the secular arena, such as public schools, they are often quick to deny it to others in the Christian arena. They don't seem to recognize their actions as an expression of elitism.

Those believers who teach that a billions-of-years-old universe and earth are compatible with the Genesis creation account and with a high view of Scripture are frequently barred from speaking in churches and in Christian schools and colleges. As I have learned from experience, my own and others', these believers are treated as having little if any-thing valuable — i.e., truthful — to say. It is as if *only* young-earth proponents deserve the pulpit or platform.

The Way Back to Reality

The fear that incites this denial of reality and this retreat to elitism must be addressed. It's a fear that runs deeper and wider than the specific case of creation time scales. Underly-ing all the so-called links between old-earth views and god-lessness is the fear that science research may someday uncover some fact about the universe, earth, or life that clearly contradicts the Bible's message. Nature may tell us something — if not long ages for the cosmos and life, some-thing else — that inescapably disagrees with what God has said in His Word. Then where will the Christian's faith be?

As long as this possibility exists in believers' minds, it will hamper their experiencing the freedom and fearlessness God makes available to us by His Spirit. "God has not given us a spirit of fear, but of power and of love and of a sound mind" (2 Timothy 1:7, NKJV). A sound mind accepts reality, physical and spiritual, not to mention emotional.

If we take the Bible seriously and literally, we see that there exists no basis for this fear. As I've stated in previous chapters, since God created the cosmos, there can never be a contradiction between what He has made and what He has spoken through the inspired writers of Scripture. The testi-mony of both will always agree, and we need never back away from facts that appear as threats. We need only study and investigate further, checking the accuracy of the facts, the accuracy of the interpretations placed on them, and the accuracy of our interpretations of God's Word and ways.

I must admit that to question and challenge brilliant, well-trained secular scientists and their myriad disciples can be intimidating, but it needn't be a futile exercise in masochism. The facts will always be on our side, even if the interpretations placed on them are not. If we adamantly defend pseudo-scientific assertions or express arrogance and disrespect, we will be shot down, and justifiably so.

My experience tells me that nonChristian audiences, presumed closed or even hostile, really may be very receptive. At one lecture I gave to high-tech engineers, more than half of the nonChristians present responded to the message by declaring their newfound commitment to Jesus Christ. I'm not suggesting the response is always this positive, but I can say it is far more positive than most people imagine.

Since I am not a particularly charismatic speaker, I can reasonably conclude that this receptivity results from the work of God's Spirit and from the strength of the scientific evidences for the God of the Bible. The latest evidences are especially potent. Let's use them for all they are worth!

CHAPTER TWELVE

Embracing the Greatest Discovery of the Century

Astronomers in the last two decades have made discoveries that carry great theological impact. The discoveries of the last two years have hit worldwide headlines more than once and have included references to God. New technical and theoretical tools have enabled astronomers to measure, for the first time, some of the most important features of the universe, of our galaxy, and of our solar system.[1] In measuring these characteristics of the creation, astronomers detect some of the Creator's characteristics. And the clues point to an awesome God.

Listed here are three recently established facts about the universe that virtually all astronomers agree on. Included is the theological significance of each, on which there is also wide agreement, even among secular scientists.

1. *Fact:* The universe is only billions of years old, not quadrillions or a near infinite number of years.

   Theological significance: Religious and philosophical systems depending on infinite or near infinite age have no foundation in reality.

2. *Fact:* The universe can be traced back to a single, ultimate origin of matter, energy, time, and space (with the dimensions of length, width, and height).

   Theological significance: The cause of the universe—i.e., the Entity (Creator) who brought the universe into existence — existed and created from outside (independent) of the matter, energy, and spacetime dimensions of the universe.

3. *Fact:* The universe, our galaxy, and our solar system exhibit more than sixty characteristics that require exquisite fine-tuning for their very existence, and also for the existence of life (any kind of physical life, not just life as we know it).

   Theological significance: The Entity (Creator) who brought the universe into existence must be personal, intelligent, powerful, and caring — personal, intelligent, and powerful, for only a super-intelligent, super-powerful Person could design and manufacture what we see, including life; caring, for only care could explain the enormous investment of creative effort, the attention to intricate detail, and the comprehensive provision for needs.

Secular Reactions

Though many nonChristian astronomers and physicists involved in making these discoveries avoid connecting them with Christianity, they nonetheless acknowledge profound theological implications (see box, page 128). Those who follow these implications to their logical ends can see that of all the so-called deities of the world's religions, only one, the God of the Bible, matches the three facts presented above.

The reason more astronomers and physicists have not made the link between their scientific discoveries and the God of the Bible has nothing to do with a deficient quantity or certainty of the evidences. But it has everything to do with their philosophical and theological ignorance or personal (sometimes moral) resistance to what their discoveries imply.

Evidence for God's Transcendence

The confidence expressed by nonChristian astrophysicists in God as the explanation for the cosmos shot up dramatically in 1992. On April 24, headlines around the globe announced

Theological Conclusions by Secular Astronomers

Since 1985 the evidences for a divinely caused and designed universe have been accumulating dramatically. Consequently, a growing number of astronomers and physicists have been making theological inferences. For example, American astronomer George Greenstein, in *The Symbiotic Universe* (1988), concluded:

> As we survey all the evidence, the thought insistently arises that some supernatural agency — or, rather, Agency — must be involved. Is it possible that suddenly, without intending to, we have stumbled upon scientific proof of the existence of a Supreme Being? Was it God who stepped in and so providentially crafted the cosmos for our benefit?[2]

British physicist Paul Davies in his 1983 book, *God and the New Physics,* denied the possibility of God as Creator and promoted an atheistic interpretation of the universe.[3] But, just one year later, his thinking had begun to change. In his 1984 book, *Superforce* , he wrote:

> The laws [of physics] . . . seem themselves to be the product of exceedingly ingenious design. . . The universe must have a purpose.[4]

In his 1988 book, *The Cosmic Blueprint,* Davies expressed further change:

> [I see] powerful evidence that there is something going on behind it all. The impression of design is overwhelming.[5]

Agnostic Robert Jastrow described the path traveled by his fellow astronomers as:

> scaling the mountains of ignorance, . . . conquering the highest peak, . . . pulling [themselves] over the final rock . . . [to be] greeted by a band of theologians who have been sitting there for centuries.[6]

observations of tiny ripples in the radiation left over from the big bang. George Smoot, project leader for the COBE experiment (Cosmic Background Explorer, the satellite that recorded these observations), declared, "What we found is evidence for the birth of the universe."[7] He added, "It's like looking at God."[8] Stephen Hawking exclaimed, "It is the discovery of the century, if not of all time."[9]

This excitement was stirred by astrophysicists' recognition of undeniable proof for the big bang model of the universe. The big bang together with the equations of general relativity tell us there must be a simultaneous beginning for all the matter, energy, and even the space-time dimensions of the universe. This beginning occurred only a few billion years ago and places the cause of the universe outside, that is, independent of, matter, energy, space, and time. Theologically this means that the Cause of the universe is independent of and transcendent to the universe. The Christian faith is the only religion among the belief systems of humankind that teaches such a doctrine about the Creator. (Several religions like Judaism, Islam, and Mormonism accept as valid at least portions of the Old and New Testaments but every one of them, outside of Christianity, denies, at least in part, God's transcendence and extra-dimensional attributes.[10])

The discoveries that led to such conclusions both came from the COBE satellite. The 1992 discovery strategically confirmed evidence that had come from the first COBE findings, reported in January 1990.[11] The earlier data showed the cosmic background radiation fit to an exceptionally high degree the energy profile of a perfectly radiating body. The data also showed that the temperature of the background radiation was very cool, less than three degrees above absolute zero, and very smooth. No irregularities in the temperature larger than one part in ten thousand could be detected.

These findings established two facts: (1) that the background radiation must come from the remote recesses of space and time, and (2) that the specific entropy of the universe must be enormous. (Entropy describes the degree to which energy in a closed system dissipates, or radiates as heat, and thus ceases to be available to perform work. *Specific* entropy is the amount of energy dissipation per proton.)

A burning candle is a good example of a highly entropic system, one that efficiently disperses energy. It has a specific entropy of about two. Only very hot explosions have much higher specific entropies. The specific entropy of the universe is enormous beyond all comparison—about one billion. No possible set of astrophysical sources, except a hot big bang, can account for such a huge specific entropy.

Yet, astronomers knew that *some* level of nonuniformity in the background radiation was needed to explain galaxy formation. Fortunately, the COBE results of 1992 were ten times more precise than the 1990 data. These newly refined measurements showed irregularities in the background radiation, confirmed at three different wavelengths, as large as about one part in a hundred thousand. The size of these irregularities is beautifully consistent with several other recent discoveries, including the first accurate measurements of the amount of ordinary and exotic matter in the universe and new revelations about the large scale structure of galaxy clusters.[12-20]

The convergence of these mutually corroborative findings gave rise to the euphoria astronomers expressed in the April 24 announcement. As University of Chicago astrophysicist Michael Turner phrased it, "We have found the Holy Grail of cosmology."[21] Many are amazed, even irritated, by the unprecedented boldness among astronomers in acknowledging the theistic implications of the big bang. According to science historian Frederic B. Burnham, the community of scientists now considers the idea that God created the universe "a more respectable hypothesis today than at any time in the last hundred years."[22]

Denial of theism among astronomers is now rare, and even the few dissenters hint at the strength of the evidence. Geoffrey Burbidge, astronomer at the University of California, San Diego, and a self-proclaimed atheist, berates his fellow astronomers for rushing to join "the First Church of Christ of the Big Bang."[23] Unfortunately, even some atheists are more able to acknowledge that the big bang implies Jesus Christ than are our young-universe creationist friends.

Can the Big Bang Imply Atheism?

A common misconception among young-universe creationists is that the big bang means a spontaneous increase of order and complexity out of primordial chaos. As such, the big bang is equated with atheism and evolutionism. To them it means God did not create the heavens and the earth. Duane Gish of the ICR goes so far as to claim that astronomers worship hydrogen gas.

As Gish and others interpret the big bang, a universe of pure hydrogen organizes itself into galaxies, stars, planets, and all the elements essential for life.[24] This progression appears to them a violation of the second law of thermodynamics (the tendency for disorder to increase with time) and thus as an affront to Christian sensibilities.[25]

What Gish and others fail to recognize is that the hydrogen which forms (by God's cause and design) one millisecond after the universe began is much more ordered and less entropic than the galaxies, stars, planets, and life-essential elements. The galaxies and stars are broken-up pieces of the primordial gas cloud. The planets and life-essential elements are the burned-up remains—i.e., ashes—of hydrogen gas. Thus, the big bang manifests, rather than violates, the second law of thermodynamics.

The problem perhaps lies in Gish's incomplete understanding of nuclear fusion. As Hans Bethe discovered in 1938, the sun and virtually all the rest of the stars in the universe are gigantic hydrogen bombs.[26-27] Like hydrogen bombs, the stars generate light and heat as their lightweight elements, such as hydrogen and helium, fuse together into heavier elements, such as carbon, nitrogen, oxygen, iron, etc. Carbon, nitrogen, and oxygen may appear to be much more ordered and complex than hydrogen, but in fact, they are nothing more than the ashes of burnt hydrogen.

So where does God fit in? He comes in both before and at the moment of the creation of the entire cosmos. He is the one who set up all the laws and constants of physics so that hydrogen forms and, after that, burns down into galaxies, stars, planets, and life-essential elements. He also intervenes along the way, personally designing and crafting a particular galaxy, star, planets, moons, and a set of heavy elements in preparation for His creation of life on one planet, Earth.

Mounting Evidence for Design

As astronomers were making "the discovery of the century," they also were measuring the universe. Until recently the universe was measureless. Now we can see and measure many of its limits and characteristics. In making these measurements, astronomers discovered the anthropic principle, the maxim that the universe has been built for humankind.

As of October 1993, twenty-five different characteristics of the universe were recognized as precisely fixed. If they were different by only slight amounts, the differences would spell the end of the existence of any conceivable life. To this list of twenty-five can be added thirty-eight characteristics of our galaxy and solar system that likewise must fall within narrowly defined ranges for life of any kind to exist.[28,29]

The degree of fine-tuning necessary for the support of life supersedes by many orders of magnitude the very best human beings have ever achieved in the design and construction of instruments, machines, or anything else. Three of the characteristics of the universe must be fine-tuned to a precision of one part in 10^{37} or better. That's supernatural!

One example of the anthropic principle may be seen in the mass density of the universe. Mass density is important because it acts as a catalyst for nuclear fusion. If the universe contained more than its approximately 10 billion-trillion stars, nuclear fusion would proceed so efficiently that all of the stars would burn up too quickly and erratically to support a planet carrying life. On the other hand, in a universe with fewer than 10 billion-trillion stars, the stars would never fuse the heavier elements—such as carbon, nitrogen, oxygen, etc.—that are essential for life chemistry. The fine-tuning of this one characteristic reveals that God's desire and care for the human race was so great that He built 10 billion-trillion stars and intricately shaped and crafted all of them, along with every other feature of the cosmos, so that at this brief moment in history we humans could survive and have a pleasant place to live.

What astronomers and physicists are discovering in these new measurements is that the Being who brought the universe into existence is not only personal, creative, powerful, and intelligent to an unimaginable degree, but He is also aware of and sensitive to the needs of humanity.

The Heavens Still Declare

The heavens have always declared the glory of God (Psalm 19:1-?) What's unique about our time is that His words spoken by the heavens are being read and understood with a degree of clarity and conviction never before possible. The greatest cosmological discoveries of the twentieth century have been made, and they are discoveries that point people to the greatest discovery of all time—the God who is there and who cares, the God who planned and prepared our existence for His good purposes.

The work of secular scientists is the friend, not the foe, of Christians. Their efforts have given us some of the strongest evidences for our Creator, God, and Savior.[30]

Let's not throw it all away. Let's share in the thrill of believers and unbelievers alike who are seeing God's glory and splendor through the things He has made and the way He has made them.

CHAPTER THIRTEEN

The Narrow Window of Time

Evolutionists and those engaged in the search for extraterrestrial intelligence share a hope and many young-universe creationists the fear that if the universe is billions of years old, life could self-assemble and develop into intelligent beings by natural processes alone. If this premise were true, life could and probably does exist elsewhere in the vastness of the cosmos.

Problems with the Premise

For a variety of reasons science tells us the premise cannot be true. As explained in chapter 7, even the entire 17-billion-year age of the universe is inadequate to explain the origin and development of life by natural processes. But the window of time for life is much narrower than 17 billion years. Only when the universe is a particular age, not too young and not too old, is life possible in it. Only when the galaxy is a particular age, not too young and not too old, is life possible in it. Only when a star is a particular age, not too young and not too old, is life possible near it. Only when a planet is a particular age, not too young and not too old, is life possible on it. Only when the moon is a particular age, not too young and not too old, is life possible near it.

These precise requirements for life mean that, though the visible universe contains about 100 billion galaxies, only a few would qualify as sites suitable for the support of life.[1] Though our galaxy contains 100 billion stars, only a few are capable of sustaining a planet on which life could exist.[2] Though our solar system contains nine planets and thousands of moons and asteroids, only on one of those bodies, planet Earth, can life survive,[3] and only if the moon[4] and Jupiter[5] have just-right dimensions and just-right positioning relative to the sun and the earth. As I have explained elsewhere,[6] these and many other factors effectively rule out the possibility, by natural means, of any other body existing in the visible universe with the capacity to support life. God could, of course, have performed His miracles of creation elsewhere than on Earth. But the Bible, though not offering any explicit statements, seems to imply that God created physical life in the universe only on planet Earth.[7]

Just Right Age of the Universe

As the universe expands from the creation event, it cools, like any other system obeying the laws of thermodynamics. When the heat energy of a system fills a greater volume, there is less heat energy per unit volume to go around. (With fifty hot coals inside your barbeque, you can cook, but if you spread those fifty coals over a football field, you're not going to warm it up much.)

For biochemical processes to operate, the universe can be neither too hot nor too cold. If it's too hot, complex molecules can't form, and if it's too cold, biochemical reactions will be too sluggish. The temperature and pressure requirements prove to be narrow. One key factor is that the temperature and pressure of the environment must be just right for liquid water to form and remain in significant quantities in just the right locations. These requirements mean that only for a few billion years in the history of the universe's expansion is there any suitable habitat for life.

An additional factor may shrink this time window for life even more, and that's nucleosynthesis. Nucleosynthesis is the process by which nucleons (protons and neutrons) are fused together to form the nuclei of heavier elements. Hydrogen requires no such fusion since its nucleus is a single proton. But oxygen, for example, requires the fusing together of eight protons and eight neutrons.

Nuclear fusion will occur only when temperature reaches a certain point: about ten million degrees.[8, 9] At temperatures much higher or lower, it won't happen.[10-12] As the universe expands and cools, it passes through the temperature range suitable for nuclear fusion in a time span of only about twenty seconds, just three-and-a-half minutes after the initial creation event. In this speck of time, approximately 24 percent of all the nucleons in the universe are fused to make helium and trace amounts of deuterium (a heavy isotope of hydrogen), lithium, boron, and beryllium. Thereafter the universe is too cool for any more fusion until stars make it possible again.

The fusion of most of the life-essential heavy elements must await the gravitational collapse of gas clouds into giant stars. Only in such collapses can the temperatures necessary for nuclear fusion ever be achieved again. And only in the cores of such giant stars can elements heavier than boron (such as carbon, nitrogen, oxygen, phosphorus, etc., the building blocks of life) be manufactured. In fact, it takes the burning up of two generations of such stars to build up a sufficient density of these heavier elements for life chemistry to become possible. That is to say, the universe must be old enough to have produced a third generation of stars but not too old, for reasons explained below. The very fact that life does exist gives us a minimum age for the universe of about 12 billion years and a maximum age of about 25 billion years.

Just Right Age of the Galaxy

Only in galaxies can the density of heavy elements ever become great enough to support life chemistry. But even in galaxies, that appropriate density of life-essential elements is achieved at one particular time only. If the galaxy is too young, not enough heavy elements will have been made yet in its stars for life chemistry to be possible. If the galaxy is too old, star and planet formation will have ceased, and no stars and planets young enough for life chemistry will exist. Only in galaxies that are older than about 10 billion years and younger than about 20 billion years will life be possible.

Just Right Age of the Star

For life on a planet to be possible, the planet must be warmed by a star that burns at a near constant brightness and color. Such stability is achieved only when the star is middle-aged. And only a star of the same mass as our star, the sun, can support a life-carrying planet.[13] For the first 100 million years after such a star begins to shine, it burns far too erratically to maintain temperatures suitable for life on an orbiting planet.[14] But after 10 billion years, hydrogen fusion at the core of such a star will cease.[15] No more hydrogen will be left. At that point the star's fusion processes will be much hotter and much more erratic. These burning phases will destroy any existing life on its planets and destroy future life chemistry processes.

Just Right Age of the Planet

For life to exist on a planet, the planet must be close enough to its star to maintain a temperature suitable for life chemistry. For advanced life to exist, the planet needs the gravitational pull of a single, large, and relatively nearby moon to stabilize the tilt of its rotation axis (otherwise it would vary too much) and to assist in the removal of greenhouse gases.[16] The planet's necessary proximity to the star and moon mean that they work as a set of brakes on the rotation period of the planet.[17] (In the case of the earth, these brakes slow the rotation period by a tiny fraction of a second each year.)

For a planet to support life, the rotation period must fit within a certain range. If the rotation period is too long, temperature differences between day and night will be too great. But if the rotation period is too short, wind velocities will increase to catastrophic levels. These findings tell us that if Earth were any younger than about 4 billion years, it would rotate too rapidly for advanced life to exist. And, if it were any older than about 6 billion years, it would rotate too slowly. Since primitive life, and especially life in the oceans, can tolerate more rapid rotation than advanced life, primitive life would have been able to survive on Earth when the planet was only 0.8 billion years old.

Middle-Age Wins

For life to exist, everything must be middle-aged. The universe, the galaxy, the star, the planet, and the moon all must be middle-aged, for in astronomy only middle-aged systems are stable.

The conclusion that *all* of the relevant bodies (the universe, our galaxy, our star, our planet, and our moon) must be a few billion years old, no more, no less, carries significant ramifications for both evolutionism and young-universe creationism. Evolutionism falls beyond the realm of possibility—for as chapter 7 explains, a few billion years is hopelessly too brief, by many orders of magnitude, to explain life's existence by strictly natural processes. Also ruled out is a time scale for the universe and the earth of only a few thousand years, for all five of the relevant bodies must be at least a billion years old (recognizing that God does not create with appearance of age) to be ready for life.

Given the laws and constants of physics that God established in the beginning, we can discover from the testimony of nature that God created physical life at the earliest possible moment. He was not dilly-dallying in His work of creation.

CHAPTER FOURTEEN

Evidence for Divine Craftsmanship

Three thousand years ago King David of Israel penned this contemplation:

> When I consider your heavens, the work of your fingers, the moon and the stars, which you have set in place, what is man that you are mindful of him, the son of man that you care for him?[1]

When David wrote, he was aware of only five other planets and about six thousand stars (the limits of unaided human vision). Today we know that the universe contains about 100 billion medium- to large-sized galaxies, each of which contains an average of 100 billion stars. The total adds up to more than 10 billion-trillion stars.

Even more stupendous to ponder is that all of the components of this vast heavenly host play an essential role in the support of life on planet Earth and of the human species in particular.[2] It takes a certain kind of galaxy for life to exist. There are even specific stars that must be specially crafted and placed in the right location of our galaxy and at the right time if any human is ever to exist and marvel at the beauty of what God has created.[3] The whole cosmos was assembled step-by-step over billions of years and across billions of trillions of miles just for us!

Humankind: The Crown of Creation

After meticulously and miraculously fashioning the cosmos, the earth, and life on the earth, the Creator culminated His masterpiece with the special creation of human beings. Here is a point on which young-universe creationists and I (and many other old-earth creationists) agree: the creation date for people. Though the biblical genealogies provide little or no help in establishing creation dates for the cosmos and Earth, I and many others agree with the young-earth creationists that they do provide a *rough* date for the advent of humanity.

I say *rough* because the Hebrew words used for father and son, *'ab* and *ben,* have broader definitions than the English translations indicate. *'Ab* sometimes refers to grandfather, great-grandfather, or great-great-grandfather, etc. Similarly, *ben* can mean son, great-grandson, etc. In the book of Daniel, Belshazzar's mother refers to Nebuchadnezzar as her son's father though, in fact, two kings separate them, and they are not even related. This flexibility in the usage of *'ab* and *ben* explains why parallel genealogies (e.g., 1 Chronicles 3, Matthew 1, Luke 3) are at variance with one another.

Even in the genealogies of Genesis 5 and 11, where the years between the birthdates of the father and the son are given, the chronology may not be as tight as it seems. Luke 3, for example, inserts at least one generation, namely Cainan, between Shelah and Arphaxad, while Genesis 11 simply records Shelah as the son of Arphaxad.

Some scholars argue that the biblical genealogies can be stretched indefinitely. Such stretching seems unwarranted by relevant biblical and scientific data. The most reliable and conservative Hebrew scholarship I have read places the biblical date for the creation of Adam and Eve between about 10,000 and 35,000 years ago (with the outside limits at about 6,000 and 60,000 years).

In Genesis 1, God speaks of *adham* (male and female), and only *adham,* as being made in His image. The point is emphasized by repetition. As humanity's story unfolds through subsequent chapters, we discover that what makes humans different is a quality called "spirit." None of the rest of Earth's creatures possesses it. By "spirit" the Bible means awareness of God and capacity to form a relationship with Him. Worship is the key evidence of the spiritual quality of the human race, and the universality of worship is evidenced in altars, temples, and religious relics of all kinds. Burial of dead, use of tools, or even painting do not qualify as evidence of the spirit, for non-spirit beings such as bower birds, elephants, and chimpanzees engage in such activities to a limited extent.

Bipedal, tool-using, large-brained primates (called hominids by anthropologists) may have roamed the earth as long ago as one million years,[4-6] but religious relics and altars date back only 8,000 to 24,000 years.[7,8] Thus, the secular archaeological date for the first spirit creatures is in complete agreement with the biblical date.

Some differences, however, between the Bible and secular anthropology remain. By the biblical definition, these hominids may have been intelligent mammals, but they were not humans. Nor did Adam and Eve physically descend from them. (According to Genesis 1:26-28 the human species was created complete and brand-new by God through His own personal miraculous intervention.) Even here, though, support from anthropology is emerging. New evidence indicates that the various hominid species may have gone extinct before, or as a result of, the appearance of modern humans.[9,10] At the very least, "abrupt transitions between [hominid] species" is widely acknowledged.[11,12]

Divine Artistry

Given that one of God's goals in creating the universe was to prepare a suitable habitat for human beings, the question sometimes arises, why did God take as long as billions of years? As preceding chapters explain, the laws of physics He designed and His plan to minimize human suffering and evil required exactly that time frame.

An added consideration arises from an altogether different perspective: the nature of creativity itself. Observe skilled sculptors, painters, or poets, artisans of any kind, and see that they always spend much more time on their masterpieces than they do on their ordinary tasks. Observe the painstaking yet joyful labor poured into each masterpiece of their design. Observe how often the artist stops to appreciate and evaluate the work in progress.

Examine the creation on any scale, from a massive galaxy to the interior of an atom, from a whale to an amoeba. The splendor of each item, its beauty of form as well as of function, speaks not of instantaneous mass production but rather of patient attention to detail, of infinite care and delight. Such delight with work in progress is expressed through Genesis 1 in the oft-repeated statement, "And God saw that it was good."

CHAPTER FIFTEEN

The Simplest Interpretation

Young-universe creationists commonly complain that interpreting the Genesis creation days as long epochs violates the plain and simple reading of the text. They conjure up the image of a humble, loving grandmother quietly studying her Bible—without the aid of Hebrew lexicons and science textbooks—and suppose that she would never, on her own, interpret the days as anything but six consecutive twenty-four-hour periods. Surely, they intimate, God would not lead this precious saint into error.

Before making any comment about this dear, hypothetical lady, I will state a personal conviction, and then recount a personal story. First, my conviction: I believe God intended that the meaning of His Word be accessible to all people, regardless of intellect or education. The Spirit of God is available to guide any active, probing mind. (He does not, however, fill the gap caused by mental laziness.) God makes the Bible (and nature, as well) comprehensible to the simplest minds and yet a challenge to the most brilliant and learned.

Next, my story.

One Case Study

I was seventeen years old when I began to study the Bible. I had heard some portions of it read aloud in my public elementary and junior high classrooms in British Columbia, and I had caught tidbits of it from my parents at home and at a United Church of Canada congregation that my family attended for several months during my childhood. But I had never studied it for myself. I had been studying science instead, which was my main interest from the time I was seven.

I started my Bible reading with the Genesis creation account. After all, it appears on the first page. I had another reason, though, for starting there. In my study of the history of astronomy, I had read dozens of creation stories from the world's religions, and I wondered if this one would be like the rest. The others were good for a few laughs, with their ludicrous descriptions and inventive disordering of events. I half anticipated that the Bible's story might be just as strange and unscientific.

My First Apologetics Discovery

What immediately caught my attention was that God established the point of view (on the surface of Earth's oceans) for the passage right at the outset, before outlining the sequence of events. This book anticipated my first concern — the perspective from which the account unfolds.

Then I made another startling observation: Along with identifying the viewpoint, Genesis 1:2 also stated Earth's initial conditions, again clarifying the context of what followed.

To be sure, not everyone would recognize these two features of the text as complementary with the scientific method. But any careful reader couldn't help but notice that they colorfully and dramatically set the scene.

With the point of view and initial conditions identified, I could proceed in my reading without relying on guesswork. In fact, after only a few minutes I understood what the text said about the order of events.

Now I was even more stunned. As far as I could tell from my limited knowledge, everything in Genesis 1, from the initial conditions to the identification and sequencing of major events made sense not only as a story but also scientifically. Never had I seen anything remotely like this in other creation accounts.

In fact, the best I had seen before were the ancient Mesopotamian creation chronicles that correctly described and ordered just two events out of more than a dozen recounted. I realized that the Bible had a perfect batting record on the ten creation events plus the initial conditions. I realized such a record required supernatural assistance. The human author could not have been guessing or presenting his own or his culture's ideas.

The discovery that Genesis might be a divinely inspired book challenged me to dig deeper into the text. I recognized that the Bible could not be taken lightly or frivolously. Though we all have different personalities, I would expect anyone spiritually open, regardless of education or intellect, to respond with similar enthusiasm to the discovery of something that looks as if it could be a message from God.

Creation Time Scale

Because Genesis 1 proved so accurate on the description and order of creation events, it seemed entirely possible to me that it might also prove true on the creation time scale. Why? Because I, like many other citizens of this century, was aware that modern astronomy has confirmed the first verse of the Bible, that the whole of the cosmos had a definite beginning, a beginning not in the extreme distant past but only a few billion years ago. Thus, when I encountered the six creation days of Genesis, it seemed possible that the word *day* could refer to longer periods than twenty-four hours. But I wasn't sure.

Trail of Clues

My first clue to some flexibility of usage for *day* was the reference to the beginning of day and night. Obviously, the word *day* here had at least two meanings.

My second clue was the use of the word *heaven* on the

second creation day. The firmament called heaven in verse 8 was distinct from the heavens of verse 1. Here again was a word taking on more than one definition. At this point I was beginning to discern that the original language of the Old Testament (Hebrew) had fewer nouns than English. Then I remembered my high school English teacher proudly pointing out that the vocabulary of English is much larger than that of most other languages.

My third clue was the lack of an evening and a morning for the seventh day. The only reason I could imagine for the author's breach of parallelism, his failure to mention the evening and morning of the seventh day, was that the day might not yet be over. When I saw that the seventh day was a day of rest for God, I recognized a possible answer to the enigma of the fossil record.

Throughout the fossil era, new species appeared one after another after another, and species went extinct, too (about one per year). But throughout the history of the human race, only the extinction rate is high. The speciation rate is negligible.

During my teenage years I had been mystified by this fact. Now I found an answer where I did not expect it—for six days God created, repeatedly and miraculously introducing new species of life on earth, but on His seventh day He ceased from His work of creating new life.

A final clue came from Genesis 2:4. There the word *day* refers to the entire creation week. It was one more piece of evidence that the Hebrew word for "day" could indeed refer to a time period other than twenty-four hours.

A Challenge That Cannot Be Ignored

That first night of serious Bible study absorbed more than two hours, and I made my way through only the first thirty-five verses. But by the time that evening had ended, I felt a remarkable exhilaration. Though not yet completely convinced that the words I was reading and all that followed were indeed the Word of God, I knew that I could not discount the possibility. Nor could I ignore the challenge to study the rest of the Bible, testing whether or not it proved similarly plausible.

I invested nearly two more years in the testing process, but that first night was a turning point. Before that night I strongly doubted that the Bible could be the error-free Word of God. After that night, I became more and more convinced that it was.

My experience is not unique. I have since learned that it characterizes the approach of many with a scientific or analytical bent. If such an individual gets through the first chapter of Genesis, unless he or she has personal (or moral) barriers to belief, that person will become a believer. If someone stumbles in that first chapter, his or her unbelief may never be overcome.

Let's turn our attention back to the humble grandmother. Not all of her peers would care enough about the issues at hand to spend two hours studying the first page of the Bible. For those who do, however, the conclusions I formed seem plain and straightforward enough. At least that's what one Arkansas grandmother (with a high school education) told me.

CHAPTER SIXTEEN

Making Sense
of Genesis 1

Ever since eighteenth-century French physician Jean Astruc first led people down the path to an implausible interpretation of the Genesis 1 creation sequence (see pages 28-29), Christians and nonChristians alike have tripped over this stumbling block. A widely held conviction that persists to this day is that the words of the biblical account and the facts of science are irreconcilably at odds.

As I have said in preceding chapters, the response to this conviction varies. Some reject the reliability of the Bible. Others reject the reliability of secular science. Still others assert that Genesis 1 and science address different kinds of truth, truth on different planes of reality, and the twain need never meet. All three groups of people make the claim that since it appears impossible to accord the description and order of creation events in Genesis 1 with the established scientific record, one might as well concede that the biblical and scientific dates for creation are at odds.

Each of the three responses reflects a logical inconsistency, something with which a persistent truth-seeker from either a Christian or a scientific background cannot be satisfied. Ironically—perhaps I should add, unwittingly—in my first night of Bible study, I picked up and used an oft-overlooked key to reconciling the text with science. Years ago I mentioned that key while conversing with a renowned seminary professor. He struck his head in amazement at something so simple, wondering how he could have missed it. He encouraged me to share it as widely as possible.

Importance of Point of View

The seeming futility of the attempt to integrate Genesis with the scientific record arises from an error in applying Galileo's rule: "Begin by establishing [not assuming] the point of view."[1] Most Bible commentaries and commentators assume the point of view to be out in the heavens looking down on the earth. As a result, they present an order for creation that echoes Astruc's and is absurd next to established science.

Ironically, Genesis 1 precisely and clearly identifies the point of view for the creation account:

> Darkness was over the surface of the deep, and the
> Spirit of God was hovering over the waters. (verse 2)

This simple statement suggests that the reader interpret the events of creation from the perspective of an observer on the surface of the earth (see figure 16.1, page 150).

The view looking upward and around from this vantage point makes a huge difference in understanding the sequence of creation events. From misplacing the perspective in the heavens, it appears that light was created after the earth. The creation of the sun, moon, and stars seems to take place after the creation of plant life and after the establishing of the water cycle. But with the point of view on the surface of the earth, looking up at the atmosphere of the earth, we recognize that God's miracles are taking place in the atmosphere of the earth, not beyond it in the galaxy and the solar system. Light was not created on the first creation day. On that day the light already created "in the beginning" suddenly broke through to the earth's surface. This breakthrough required the transformation of the atmosphere (plus the interplanetary medium) from opaque to translucent. On the fourth creation day we see yet another atmospheric transformation, this time from translucent to transparent. Through that transformation, the sun, moon, and stars became visible for the first time on Earth's surface. It's not that God made (or created) them on the fourth day; He simply made them visible and distinguishable on that day.

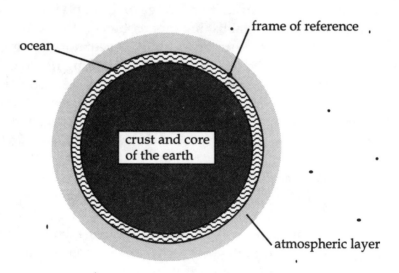

Figure 16.1: The Point of View for Genesis 1
The point of view from which the Genesis 1 creation events are described is from the perspective of an observer on the surface of the ocean, underneath the cloud layer, as implied in the second verse.

Verse 16 reads, "God made two great lights. . . . He also made the stars." This sentence follows the opening statement for the fourth creation day (verse 14), "Let there be lights in the expanse of the sky," and is a parenthetical note indicating that these heavenly bodies had been formed sometime in the past.

In the Hebrew language there are just three verb forms analogous to the verb tenses of the English language: (a) a verb form to express commands, (b) a verb form for action not yet complete, and (c) a verb form for action completed at some time in the past.[2-3] The verb, *'asah,* translated "made" in verse 16, is in the verb form connoting completed action. Thus the sun, moon, and stars either were made on the fourth day, the third day, the second day, the first day, or in the beginning. The latter must be the correct timing since the heavens and earth (*shamayim erets*) of verse 1 includes the entire physical universe of galaxies, stars, planets, etc.[4]

With the point of view fixed on the earth's surface, the "dark," "formless," and "empty" initial conditions make sense. It is dark in spite of the already existing heavens and earth because the earth's primordial atmosphere and the solar system's primordial interplanetary debris prevent the light of the sun, moon, and stars from reaching the surface of the earth. The earth's surface is empty of life and unfit for life, because without light photosynthesis is impossible.

Lest anyone think that this interpretation of the point of view and the initial conditions is unique to me, and therefore suspect, let me remind the reader that Old Testament scholar and Hebrew linguist Gleason Archer made the same discovery in 1955, seven years before I did.[5] Robert Newman, John Snow, Herman Eckelmann, William Henry Green, and Daniel Wonderly, all with advanced degrees in science, theology, or both, published a similar interpretation of Genesis 1 in 1977.[6]

Creation Events and the Fossil Record

With the point of view and initial conditions correctly identified, the sequence of Genesis creation events no longer seems difficult to harmonize with the record of astronomy, paleontology, geology, and biology. The few purported conflicts with the fossil record stem from inaccurate interpretations of some Hebrew nouns for various plant and animal species.

For example, some have ridiculed Genesis for declaring that insects appear late in the record of life on earth, *after* the birds and sea mammals and just before human beings. The problem reference is to the creatures "that creepeth upon the earth" (Genesis 1:25-26, KJV). The Hebrew word in question is *remes,* and its broad definition encompasses rapidly moving vertebrates, such as rodents, hares, and lizards. But *remes* in verse 24 has a more restricted usage. The creatures under discussion are the *nephesh* (verses 20-25)—soulish creatures, creatures that can relate to humans; creatures with qualities of mind, will, and emotion. These can only be birds and mammals. So the *remes* of verse 24 cannot be insects or even reptiles. They must be short-legged land mammals such as rodents and hares.

Another point of ridicule is the mention of land mammals (Genesis 1:25) as part of the sixth creation day, while sea mammals (1:21) show up on the fifth creation day. The fossil record clearly shows that the first sea mammals came on the scene after the first land mammals. The answer to this ridicule comes from identifying the kinds of creatures (the *chayyah,* the *behemah,* and the *remes*) the text associates with the sixth creation day (1:25). The words refer not to all the land mammals but rather to three specific classes of land mammals:

1. Long-legged quadruped usually described as wild
2. Long-legged quadruped that is easy to tame
3. Short-legged quadruped

Apparently, these particular land mammals were designed to coexist with human beings. The fossil record confirms that such land mammals do not show up until after the initial appearance of birds and sea mammals.

Events of the third creation day have also been challenged. The Hebrew phrase translated as "seeds, trees, and fruit" (Genesis 1:11-12) has been taken by some as a reference to deciduous plants. However, the respective Hebrew nouns, *zera', 'ets,* and *periy* are generic terms that easily can be applied to plant species as primitive as those that appeared at the beginning of the Cambrian era (c 500,000,000 years ago). Their early mention in the Genesis creation account poses no scientific problem.

Scientific evidence for ocean life predating land life poses no threat either. The Spirit of God "brooded" over the face of the waters (Genesis 1:2), possibly creating life in the oceans before the events of the six creation days begin.

Order of Creation Conditions and Events

Clearly, a detailed comparison of the Genesis creation account with nature's record requires careful study of the Hebrew words in their context. This study, however, leads not to scientific impasse, but rather to powerful evidence of the scientific soundness of the Bible. Such soundness cannot be a lucky fluke. Given that it was recorded more than 3,400 years ago, the book of Genesis must be supernaturally inspired.

Table 16.1: Order of Genesis 1 Events

1. Creation by God's fiat miracle of the entire physical universe (length, width, height, time, matter, energy, galaxies, stars, planets, etc.).
   Note: Planet Earth is empty of life and unfit for life; Earth's primordial atmosphere and the solar system's interplanetary debris prevent the light of the sun, moon, and stars from reaching the surface of the earth's ocean.
2. Clearing of the interplanetary debris and partial transformation of the earth's atmosphere so that light from the heavenly bodies now penetrates to the surface of the earth's ocean.
3. Formation of water vapor in the troposphere under conditions that establish a stable water cycle.
4. Formation of continental land masses together with ocean basins.
5. Production of plants on the continental land masses.
6. Transformation of the atmosphere from a translucent condition to one that is at least occasionally transparent.
7. Production of swarms of small sea animals.
8. Creation by God's fiat miracles of sea mammals and birds.
9. Creation by God of land mammals capable of interacting with the future human race.
10. Creation by God's fiat miracle of the human species.

Completing the analysis of words and contexts[7] yields the list of creation events seen in table 16.1 (page 153). Obviously, no author writing more than 3,400 years ago, as Moses did, could have so accurately described and sequenced these events, plus the initial conditions, without divine assistance. And if God could guide the words of Moses to scientific and historical precision in this most complex report of divine activity, we have reason to believe we can trust Him to communicate with perfection through all the other Bible writers as well.

Biblical Creationism

Genesis 1 is not the only chapter in the Bible that describes the manner in which God created the realm of nature. Genesis 2, Job 38–39, Psalm 104, Proverbs 8:22-31, John 1:1-5, Colossians 1:15-17, and Hebrews 11:3 also address God's creative activity. From all these passages it is possible to develop a consistent position on how God created. It is stated concisely here:

> The God of the Bible generated the universe transcendently, that is, independent of matter, energy, and the dimensions of length, width, height, and time. He personally designed and built the universe and our solar system so that life could flourish on Earth. Though the Bible does not identify the specific means by which God produced the lower life-forms, it does state that He specially created through fiat, miraculous means birds, mammals, and human beings. Since the time these animal kinds were created by God, they have been subject to minor changes in accordance with the laws of nature, which God established. However, the Bible clearly denies that any of these species descended from lower forms of life. Human beings are distinct from all other animals, including the bipedal primates that preceded them, in that humans alone possess body, soul, and spirit.

CHAPTER SEVENTEEN

Attempt
at Reconciliation

By the early 1970s, the supposed irreconcilability of Genesis 1 (and other portions of Scripture) with the scientific record was giving impetus to revision of the long-held views of biblical authority and inerrancy. Several evangelical scholars and seminaries proposed that the word *infallible* replace the word *inerrant* as the appropriate adjective for the Word of God. *Infallible* would mean that Scripture is wholly trustworthy on matters of Christian faith and practice, while not necessarily on matters of science, history, and geography. This term change seemed only reasonable to some Christian leaders, but to others it seemed an unnecessary and dangerous concession.

Inerrancy Upheld

In an attempt to counter the revision movement, in 1977 a group of Christian scholars founded the International Council on Biblical Inerrancy (ICBI). The council's primary purpose was to defend and apply the doctrine of biblical inerrancy as "an essential element for the authority of Scripture and a necessity for the health of the church."[1] It also existed to "counter the drift from this important doctrinal foundation by significant segments of evangelicalism and the outright denial of it by other church movements."[2]

Initial ICBI sessions focused on defining inerrancy. Then the group began to tackle some of the issues directly challenging scriptural authority. The 1982 ICBI Summit discussed at length the matter of the ages of the universe and the earth.

Summit on Scripture and Natural Science

Three full-length papers were presented at the 1982 Summit. First, Walter Bradley, professor of mechanical engineering (a former advocate of the young-universe perspective), presented the case for interpreting the Genesis creation days as long epochs. Next, Henry Morris, founder and president of the Institute for Creation Research, presented the case for six consecutive twenty-four-hour creation days. Finally, Gleason Archer, professor of Old Testament and Semitics (Semitic languages and culture, including Hebrew), presented his analysis of the original language of the Genesis text.

After presentation of these papers, the scholars in attendance, mostly theologians, deliberated over them for many hours. Afterward, the group concluded that adherence to six consecutive twenty-four-hour creation days is nonessential to belief in biblical inerrancy. The Summit participants then framed the following set of affirmations and denials with respect to natural science. All but Morris signed it.

ICBI Affirmations and Denials on Scripture and Natural Science[3]

We *affirm* that any preunderstandings which the interpreter brings to Scripture should be in harmony with scriptural teaching and subject to correction by it.

We *deny* that Scripture should be required to fit alien preunderstandings, inconsistent with itself, such as naturalism, evolutionism, scientism, secular humanism, and relativism.

We *affirm* that since God is the author of all truth, all truths, biblical and extrabiblical, are consistent and cohere, and that the Bible speaks truth when it touches on matters pertaining to nature, history, or anything else. We further affirm that in some cases extrabiblical data have value for clarifying what Scripture teaches, and for prompting correction of faulty interpretations.

We *deny* that extrabiblical views ever disprove the teaching of Scripture or hold priority over it.

We *affirm* the harmony of special with general revelation and therefore of biblical teaching with the facts of nature.

We *deny* that any genuine scientific facts are inconsistent with the true meaning of any passage of Scripture.

We *affirm* that Genesis 1-11 is factual, as is the rest of the book.

We *deny* that the teachings of Genesis 1-11 are mythical and that scientific hypotheses about earth history or the origin of humanity may be invoked to overthrow what Scripture teaches about creation.

Attempt at Reconciliation

When it became evident that Morris would not accept any statement short of a flat denial of *any* possibility for a creation time scale longer than a few thousand years, the ICBI agreed to word their affirmations and denials in a way that would not condemn any position on the dates for creation. In the council's opinion, belief in biblical inerrancy required no immutable assertion of the cosmic or geologic ages. Belief in a finite date for creation was viewed as sufficient.

By refraining from dogmatic statements on the creation date, the ICBI hoped to keep the creation time scale from becoming an issue for inerrancy, doctrinal orthodoxy, evangelism, and missions.

Sadly, their hope has not been fulfilled. One reason is

that the council's deliberations, affirmations, and denials regarding Scripture and natural science received insufficient publicity within the evangelical community to make a significant impact. Something more was and still is needed.

CHAPTER EIGHTEEN

New Proposal
for Lasting Peace

Though young-universe creationists have had little success in converting secular scientists to their view, they certainly have made inroads among new converts to the Christian faith. A personal story comes to mind.

After giving a lecture at the California Institute of Technology on scientific evidences supporting the Christian faith, I met a biology student who had three weeks earlier committed his life to Jesus Christ. He described his initial burst of joy and gratitude over his newfound life and purpose. He was ready to do whatever his Savior asked.

Almost immediately he met some fellow Christians who happened to be young-universe creationists. They insisted that the price of his salvation was denial of the billions-of-years age of the cosmos and the earth, and with it all the foundational principles of astronomy, physics, geology, chemistry, and paleontology. They backed their case with this Bible passage: "If anyone comes to me and does not hate his father and mother, his wife and children, his brothers and sisters—yes, even his own life—he cannot be my disciple. And anyone who does not carry his cross and follow me cannot be my disciple" (Luke 14:26-27). Wanting to obey God at all cost, this young man determined to do what these "wiser" believers said he must, even if it meant living a double life. He would resist the temptation during his work and study time to believe that the universe is real, and at church he would practice his new belief that it is an illusion or a mirage.

In response to my message and others' encouragement, he let go of the burden of a double life, of believing yet trying not to believe the reality his studies revealed. He saw that believing the Bible did not require the sacrifice of his rational mind. Sharing his faith with friends would now be possible for him, even enjoyable. He expressed profound relief, and he said he found new meaning in the motto of Caltech, "The truth shall make you free" (John 8:32, KJV).

I have met many other believers who do not yet know this young man's freedom and joy. Having paid the price they were taught they must pay, they insist that no one should be let off any easier. Every respectable Christian must deny the facts of science. The result? A burdensome walk with God (hardly the exhortations of Matthew 11:25 and Ephesians 2:8-10), or an unhealthy disconnection from reality. What a terrible choice! And what awful advertising, if I may use that term, for Christianity.

The Council at Jerusalem

An analogous problem to the young-universe versus old-universe issue arose in the early days of the church. Gentiles were rapidly responding to the witness of Jews who believed in Jesus as their Messiah-Redeemer. But this historic evangelistic breakthrough soon met with a major obstacle. In Acts 15:1 we read, "Some men came down from Judea to Antioch and were teaching the brothers: 'Unless you are circumcised according to the custom taught by Moses, you cannot be saved.'" As the text records, a sharp dispute broke out. Thank God, the church responded wisely and graciously.

Paul and Barnabas, leaders of the Gentile Christians, were sent to Jerusalem to appeal to the Jewish leaders of the church. The council listened as Paul and Barnabas testified of the miraculous way Gentiles were coming to faith in Jesus

Christ. Peter added a reminder that it is through grace, not works, that anyone is saved, including the Jews. As the first apostle to lead Gentiles to Christ (in the home of the Roman centurion, Cornelius—Acts 10), Peter's opinion was especially important. The council deliberated, and then James, the leader of the Jerusalem church, made this decisive statement: "We should not make it difficult for the Gentiles who are turning to God" (Acts 15:19). He recommended that a letter be written exhorting the Gentiles to adhere to those few basics that were essential for salvation and growth in Christ. The council concurred.

The Letter About Essentials

Thus, a letter was sent out to all the Gentile congregations, setting them free from the requirement of circumcision and encouraging them with these words, "It seemed good to the Holy Spirit and to us not to burden you with anything beyond the following requirements" (Acts 15:28). The short list included abstinence from sexual immorality and other practices of pagan worship. As a result of this letter, a potential rift was avoided, the Gentile believers were overjoyed, and evangelism flourished.

Contributing to the letter's success was the unanimity behind it, the respect it expressed for Paul and Barnabas, and its avoidance of condemnation toward those who promoted circumcision as essential. Words such as "one accord" (Acts 15:25, NKJV) communicated that the council participants were undivided. The conflict would not come back again to haunt the Gentiles.

The council's personal endorsement of Paul and Barnabas settled the questions about their character, testimony, teaching, and ministry raised by the slanderous accusations from the circumcision party. The reference to "our beloved Barnabas and Paul" (Acts 15:25, NKJV) spoke volumes of reassurance.

The emphasis on Barnabas and Paul's courage, as "men who risked their lives for the name of our Lord Jesus Christ"

(Acts 15:26), helped blunt the charge that Paul, Barnabas, and their followers were appeasing the Gentiles on the circumcision issue to avoid persecution. The label "coward" could hardly stick to men whose outreach efforts brought them repeated imprisonment, flogging, and death threats from both Jews and Gentiles, as the Jerusalem Council acknowledged.[1]

The council decided that the circumcision party was in error. It supported the work of Paul, Barnabas, and others, refuting the necessity for circumcision. But the council refrained from humiliating and rejecting those who promoted the error. Gentle correction offered compassionately, along with recognition of the fruit of Paul and Barnabas's ministry, ultimately eased tensions and turned some of these people around. Harsh condemnation would have deepened the rift and heightened the intransigence.

As it was, the ferocity of the circumcision party initially increased. Several dissenters lost their lives as a result (see Acts 21:27-36, 22:22, 23:12-30, 25:1-12). But time, as well as wisdom, was on the council's side. The Gentile segment of the church survived. In fact, the letter widened the door for Gentiles to enter the Christian community. And as more and more Gentiles joined the church, the strength of the circumcision party diminished. By the end of the first century, circumcision was no longer an issue, and it hasn't been since.

A Proposal

Much as circumcision divided the first-century church, I see the creation date issue dividing the church of this century. As circumcision distorted the gospel and hampered evangelism, so, too, does young-universe creationism.

Current scientific research is a God-given tool for building faith in Christ and in His Word—a tool we would do well to keep and to use. The young-earth party unwittingly seeks to toss it out and destroy its potential for impact. The receptivity of secular "rationalists" (I use the term in a practical sense, rather than in the technical, philosophical sense) to scientific evidences for the Christian faith can be described only as phenomenal. My own and others' experience attests to it. These open-hearted people respect science and sometimes are scientists and, at the same time, also want to grow in knowledge of God and in faith. However, they are not being welcomed, accepted, understood, or appreciated in the church, at least not in most congregations. We seem unprepared to receive them.

A crying need on the part of the entire Christian community is to face the age-of-the-universe (and the earth) issue head on and to resolve it in the spirit exemplified by the Jerusalem council. I'm committed to do everything in my power to promote the formation of such a council — one that includes not only seminary professors, but also pastors, missionaries, scientists, and leaders of parachurch and missions organizations. Sponsorship of this council by a widely respected organization, with grants from many sources for expenses, may be a means of guaranteeing the highest level of participation.

I envision the goals of this new council to parallel those of the first-century Jerusalem council. Specifically, I would recommend the following five steps of action:

1. A report on and acknowledgment of the unprecedented fruitfulness of outreach to secular rationalists using the facts of nature to establish the truthfulness of the words of the Bible.
2. A recognition of science and scientific investigation as an ally of the Christian faith, not an enemy.
3. A presentation of relevant scientific and biblical data on the creation dates for the universe, the earth, the solar system, the various life-forms evident in the fossil record, and human beings, along with discussion of the means of creation.
4. A consideration of which creation doctrines are essential for the Christian faith and which are not.
5. Preparation of a statement to all churches, mission

agencies, and parachurch organizations within the evangelical community. This statement would include:

- An endorsement of biblical inerrancy, with a review of that term's definition and application, and a summary of objective evidences supporting it.
- An acknowledgment that the facts of nature provide valuable tools for demonstrating the truth of the Bible and for helping believers to correct or clarify some interpretations of the words of the Bible.
- A report on the fruitfulness of those who have used the facts of nature to lead secularists to faith in Jesus Christ, with a recognition of their courage in testifying before unbelievers.
- An expression of commendation to young-earth and old-earth creationists alike who have demonstrated integrity and boldness in standing up for morality and Christian values.
- The beliefs about science, faith, and creation that are essential for Christian life and growth and maintenance of biblical inerrancy.
- An expression of appreciation and respect for scientists, whose rigorous investigation of nature adds to our knowledge and understanding of truth.
- A commitment to pursue open dialogue and research integrating scientific facts and the words of the Bible, with the goal of establishing more truth about God's creation and God's Word to us.

The overriding purpose of this council is removal of the "secular rationalists not welcome" sign invisibly posted on the doors of Christian gatherings of all kinds. As we see more of these people coming to Christ and get to know what they are like, we can adapt to their needs, interests, and learning styles in the way our churches conduct their ministries.

To denounce young-universe creationists in the process

would be a grave error. It would be far better to remove the anti-science, anti-intellectual bias from Christian churches, schools, and organizations. Far better to take positive steps—such as developing study, discussion, and research groups for seekers in a nonecclesiastical setting—to encourage the active participation of facts-and-logic personality types.

Once these people become as well represented in the evangelical community as they are in society at large, the creation-date controversy will doubtless evaporate. The stumbling block will disappear. Perhaps the greatest benefit of scientists' (and scientific thinkers') involvement in Christian fellowships could be their strategic assistance in fulfilling Christ's commission to the church. With their training and perspective, they could help equip thousands of Christians to share their faith effectively in an increasingly secularized world. To win these people to Christ and to welcome them to participate in our church ministries is to pave the way for the greatest ingathering the church has ever seen.

Notes

Introduction

1. Gallup, George, "Creation/Evolution Debate Goes On," *Los Angeles Times Syndicate*, quoted in *The Sacramento Bee*, 28 August 1982, page B7.
2. Scott, Eugenie C., "Gallup Reports High Level of Belief in Creationism," *National Center for Science Education Reports*, vol. 13, no. 3 (1993), page 9.

One: What's All the Fuss About?

1. Ross, Hugh, *The Creator and the Cosmos* (Colorado Springs, CO: Nav-Press, 1993).
2. Buswell, James; Gish, Duane; Ross, Hugh; Saucy, Robert; and Willard, Dallas, "Speakers' Panel on Genesis," *Science & Genesis*, lecture series sponsored by The Institute of Apologetics in the Study of Christianity held at Rolling Hills Estates Covenant Church, Rolling Hills Estates, Calif., 12 December 1988.
3. Ross, Hugh, *What Is Christianity?* fourth edition (Pasadena, CA: Reasons To Believe, 1980).
4. Ross, Hugh, *Genesis One: A Scientific Perspective*, second edition (Pasadena, CA: Reasons To Believe, 1983).
5. Allen, Steve, *Steve Allen on the Bible, Religion, & Morality* (Buffalo, NY: Prometheus Books, 1990), pages 19-20.
6. Hazen, Robert M., and Trefil, James, *Science Matters: Achieving Scientific Literacy* (New York: Doubleday, 1990), page 243. (Hazen and Trefil may not be secular humanists, but they do provide brief summaries of the stated positions of secular humanists on creationism.)
7. Birx, H. James, *Interpreting Evolution: Darwin & Teilhard de Chardin* (Buffalo, NY: Prometheus Books, 1991), page 98.
8. Hazen and Trefil, page 244.
9. Johnson, Phillip E., *Darwin on Trial* (Washington, DC: Regnery Gateway, 1991), page 141.
10. Ruse, Michael, *Darwinism Defended: A Guide to the Evolution Controversies* (Reading, MA: Addison-Wesley, 1982), pages 303, 321.
11. Morris, Henry M., and Morris, John D., *Science, Scripture, and the Young Earth* (El Cajon, CA: Institute for Creation Research, 1989), page 67.
12. Akridge, Russell, "A Recent Creation Interpretation of the Big Bang and Expanding Universe," *Bible-Science Newsletter* (May 1982), pages 1, 4.

Two: Interpretations of Early Church Leaders

1. Taylor, Ian T., *In the Minds of Men: Darwin and the New World Order* (Toronto: TFE Publishing, 1984), pages 283-285.
2. Morris, Henry, "The Compromise Road," *Impact* 177 (El Cajon, CA: Institute for Creation Research, March 1988), page ii.
3. DeYoung, Donald B., "Christianity and the Age of the Earth," *Grace Theological Journal* 4.2 (1983), page 298.
4. Philo, Judaeus of Alexandria, "De Opificio Mundi" (On the Account of the World's Creation Given by Moses), *Philo*, vol. I, trans. F. H. Colson and G. H. Whitaker (London: William Heinemann and Cambridge, MA: Harvard University Press, 1949), page 13.
5. Philo, Judaeus of Alexandria, "Legum Allegoria" (Allegorical Interpretations of Genesis II., III., Book I, section 2), in *Philo*, vol. I, pages 146-149.
6. Josephus, Flavius, "The Antiquities of the Jews," *The Life and Works of Flavius Josephus*, trans. William Whiston (Philadelphia: John C. Winston, 1957), page 32.
7. Justin Martyr, "Dialogue With Trypho, chapter 81," *Writings of Saint Justin Martyr*, in *The Fathers of the Church*, vol. 6, Ludwig Schopp, editorial director (New York: Christian Heritage, 1948), pages 277-278.
8. Irenaeus, "Against Heresies," Book V, Chapter XXIII, Section 2, *The Ante-Nicene Fathers*, vol. I, ed. Alexander Roberts and James Donaldson (Grand Rapids, MI: Eerdmans, 1981), pages 551-552.
9. Irenaeus, pages 551-552.
10. Clement of Alexandria, "The Stromata, Book VI," *Clement of Alexandria: A Study in Christian Platonism and Gnosticism*, by Salvatore R. C. Lilla (Oxford: Oxford University Press, 1971), pages 198-199.
11. Clement of Alexandria, "The Stromata, Book VI, Chapter XVI," *The Ante-Nicene Fathers*, vol. II, pages 512-514.
12. Clement of Alexandria, page 513.
13. Origen, *Origen on First Principles*, Book IV, Chapters I and II, trans. G. W. Butterworth, introduction by Henri De Lubac (New York: Harper Torchbooks, Harper and Row, 1966), pages 277-278.
14. Origen, "Against Celsus," Book VI, Chapter LX, in *The Ante-Nicene Fathers*, vol. IV, ed. Alexander Roberts and James Donaldson (Grand Rapids, MI: Eerdmans, 1979), pages 600-601.
15. Origen, "Homilies on Genesis and Exodus," trans. Ronald E. Heine, *The Fathers of the Church*, vol. 71, Hermigild Dressler, editorial director (Washington, DC: Catholic University of America Press, 1982), page 48.
16. Origen, *Origen on First Principles*, Book IV, Chapter III, page 288.
17. Origen, "Against Celsus," Book VI, Chapter LXI, in *The Ante-Nicene Fathers*, vol. IV, page 601.
18. Lactantius, "The Divine Institutes, Book VII, Chapter XIV," in *The Ante-Nicene Fathers*, vol. VII, page 211.
19. Victorinus of Pettau, "The Created World, Book VI," in *The Ante-Nicene Fathers*, vol. VII, page 342.
20. Methodius of Olympus, "Fragment," in *The Ante-Nicene Fathers*, vol. VI,

page 310.

21. Augustinus, Aurelius, Bishop of Hippo, "The City of God, Book XI, Chapter 6," in *The Fathers of the Church*, vol. 14, Roy Joseph Defferrari, editorial director (New York: Fathers of the Church, Inc., 1952), page 196.

22. Augustinus, Aurelius, Bishop of Hippo, "The Literal Meaning of Genesis, Book Five, Chapter 2," in *Ancient Christian Writers: The Works of the Fathers in Translation*, ed. Johannes Quasten, Walter J. Burghardt, and Thomas C. Lawler, no. 41, St. Augustine, *The Literal Meaning of Genesis*, translated and annotated by John Hammond Taylor, vol. I, books 1-6 (New York: Newman Press, 1982), page 148.

23. Augustinus, Aurelius, Bishop of Hippo, "The Literal Meaning of Genesis, Book Four, Chapter 27," in *Ancient Christian Writers: The Works of the Fathers in Translation*, no. 41, St. Augustine, *The Literal Meaning of Genesis*, page 135.

24. Augustinus, Aurelius, Bishop of Hippo, "The Literal Meaning of Genesis, Book Four, Chapter 28," in *Ancient Christian Writers: The Works of the Fathers in Translation*, no. 41, St. Augustine, *The Literal Meaning of Genesis*, page 136.

25. Augustinus, Aurelius, Bishop of Hippo, "The Confessions, Book XIII, Section 51," in *The Fathers of the Church*, vol. 21, trans. Vernon J. Bourke (New York: Fathers of the Church, Inc., 1953), page 455.

26. Eusebius, Bishop of Caesarea, *Preparation for the Gospel, Part 1, Books 1-9*, trans. Edwin Hamilton Gifford (Grand Rapids, MI: Baker Book House, 1981), page 343.

27. Eusebius, Bishop of Caesarea, *Preparation for the Gospel, Part 2, Books 10-15*, trans. Edwin Hamilton Gifford (Grand Rapids, MI: Baker Book House, 1981), page 603.

28. Basil, Bishop of Caesarea, "The Hexaemeron," *A Select Library of Nicene and Post-Nicene Fathers of the Christian Church, second services*, ed. Philip Schaff and Henry Wace, vol. VIII, *St. Basil: Letters and Select Works; The Nine Homilies of the Hexaemeron and the Letters of Saint Basil the Great*, Archbishop of Caesarea, trans. Blomfield Jackson (Grand Rapids, MI: Eerdmans, 1955), page 55.

29. Basil, Bishop of Caesarea, page 64.

30. Ambrose, Bishop of Milan, "Saint Ambrose: Hexameron," trans. John J. Savage, *The Fathers of the Church, A New Translation*, vol. 42, Roy Joseph Deferrari, et al. (New York: Fathers of the Church, Inc., 1961), page 42.

31. Ambrose, Bishop of Milan, pages 42-43.

32. Ambrose, Bishop of Milan, page 43.

Three: The Gathering Storm

1. Ussher, James, Archbishop of Armagh, *Annalis Veteris Testamenti* (Londini: J. Flesher, 1650–1654). For the same book in English, see Ussher, James, Archbishop of Armagh, *The Annals of the World* (London: E. Tyler for J. Crook and G. Bedell, 1658).

2. Brewater, E. T., *Creation: A History of Non-Evolutionary Theories* (1927),

page 109; quoted in Ramm, Bernard, *The Christian View of Science and Scripture* (Grand Rapids, MI: Eerdmans, 1955), page 174.

3. Johnson, Paul, *A History of Christianity* (New York: Atheneum, 1976), page 413.
4. Ramm, Bernard, *The Christian View of Science and Scripture* (Grand Rapids, MI: Eerdmans, 1955), pages 188-190.
5. Osgood, Howard, "Jean Astruc," *Presbyterian and Reformed Review* 3 (1892), page 87.
6. Astruc, Jean, *Conjectures sur les mémoirs originaux dont il parait que Moise s'est servi pour composer la Genèse, avec des remarques qui appuient ou éclaircissens ces conjectures* (Bruxelles: Fricx, 1953), pages 378, 439.
7. O'Doherty, Eamonn, "The Conjectures of Jean Astruc, 1753," *Catholic Biblical Quarterly* 15 (1953), pages 300-304.
8. Gosse, Philip Henry, *Omphalos: An Attempt to Untie the Geological Knot* (London: John Van voorst, Paternoster Row, 1857), pages 290-297, 335.
9. Gosse, pages 341-351.

Four: The Winds of War

1. Siemens, David F., "The Conflict Between Christianity and Biological Science," *Journal of the American Scientific Association* (March 1966), page 5. The wording varies in the accounts of the incident since no notes were taken and people's memories differ.
2. Editorial Staff at the Catholic University of America, Washington, DC, *New Catholic Encyclopedia*, vol. 6 (New York: McGraw-Hill, 1967), page 223.
3. Levine, Lawrence W., *Defender of the Faith: William Jennings Bryan: The Last Decade, 1915-1925* (New York: Oxford University Press, 1965), page 349.
4. Welch, Claude A., et al., *Biological Science: Molecules to Man* (Boston: Houghton Mifflin, 1968), pages 43-676.
5. Whitcomb, J. C., Jr., and Morris, H. M., *The Genesis Flood* (Philadelphia: Presbyterian and Reformed, 1961).
6. Broad, William J., "Louisiana Puts God into Biology Lessons," *Science* 213 (1981), pages 628-629.
7. Lewin, Roger, "A Response to Creationism Evolves," *Science* 214 (1981), pages 635-638.
8. Lewin, Roger, "Creationism Goes on Trial in Arkansas," *Science* 214 (1981), pages 1101-1104.
9. Lewin, Roger, "Creationism on the Defense in Arkansas," *Science* 215 (1982), pages 33-34.
10. Lewin, Roger, "Judge's Ruling Hits Hard at Creationism," *Science* 215 (1982), pages 381-384.
11. Overton, William, "Creationism in Schools: The Decision in McLean Versus the Arkansas Board of Education," *Science* 215 (1982), pages 934-943.
12. Skow, John, "Creationism as Social Movement: The Genesis of Equal Time," *Science 81*, vol. 2, no. 10 (1981), pages 54-60.

13. Hammond, Allen, and Magulis, Lynn, "Creationism as Science: Farewell to Newton, Einstein, Darwin . . . ," *Science 81*, vol. 2, no. 10 (1981), pages 55-57.

14. Skow, John, "What Do the Creationists Say?" *Science 81*, vol. 2, no. 10 (1981), page 60.

15. Lewin, "A Response to Creationism Evolves," pages 635-638.

16. McCollister, Betty, ed., *Voices For Evolution* (Berkeley, CA: National Center For Science Education, 1989), page iv.

17. Blick, Edward F., *Special Creation Vs. Evolution* (Oklahoma City, OK: Southwest Radio Church, 1981), pages 2-11.

18. Morris, Henry M., *Scientific Creationism*, general edition (San Diego, CA: Creation Life Publishers, 1974), page 255.

19. Jukes, Thomas, quoted by Roger Lewin, "A Response to Creationism Evolves," *Science* 214 (1981), page 638.

20. Bambach, Richard K., "Responses to Creationism," *Science* 220 (1983), page 852.

21. Gallup, George, "Creation/Evolution Debate Goes On," *Los Angeles Times Syndicate*, quoted in *The Sacramento Bee*, 28 August 1982, page B7.

22. North, Gary, *The Dominion Covenant: Genesis* (Tyler, TX: Institute for Christian Economics, 1987), pages 254-255.

23. Editors, "Morris Debates for Young Earth at Wheaton," *Acts & Facts*, Institute for Creation Research, vol. 15, no. 8 (1986), page 5.

24. Lubenow, Marvin, "Does a Proper Interpretation of Scripture Require a Recent Creation?" *Impact* 65, Institute for Creation Research (1978), page iv.

25. Whitcomb, John C., Jr., *The Early Earth* (Grand Rapids, MI: Baker Book House, 1972), page 29.

26. Whitcomb, page 30.

27. Dolphin, Lambert, *Jesus: Lord of Time and Space* (Green Forest, AR: New Leaf Press, 1988), page 204.

28. Dolphin, page 205.

29. Petersen, Dennis R., *Unlocking the Mysteries of Creation* (South Lake Tahoe, CA: Christian Equippers International, 1986), page 23.

30. Whitcomb, John C., and DeYoung, Donald B., *The Moon: Its Creation, Form, and Significance* (Winona Lake, IN: BMH Books, 1978), page 69.

31. Morris, Henry, "The Compromise Road," *Impact 177*, March 1988 (El Cajon, CA: Institute for Creation Research, 1988), page iv.

32. North, page 417.

33. Morris, John D., "Should a Church Take a Stand on Creation?" *Back to Genesis* 41 (El Cajon, CA: Institute for Creation Research, May 1992), page d.

Five: Biblical Basis for Long Creation Days

1. Wilson, William, *Old Testament Word Studies* (Grand Rapids, MI: Kregel Publications, 1978), page 109.

2. Brown, Francis; Driver, S. R.; and Briggs, Charles A., *A Hebrew and English Lexicon of the Old Testament* (Oxford, UK: Clarendon Press,

1968), pages 787-788.
3. Harris, R. Laird; Archer, Gleason L.; and Waltke, Bruce K., *Theological Wordbook of the Old Testament*, vol. II (Chicago: Moody, 1980), page 694.
4. Brown, Driver, and Briggs, pages 133-134.
5. Harris, Archer, and Waltke, *Theological Wordbook of the Old Testament*, vol. I, page 125.
6. Wilson, page 109.
7. Calvin, Jean, *Commentaries on the Twelve Minor Prophets, Voume I: Hosea*, trans. John Owen (Edinburgh, UK: The Calvin Translation Society, 1846), pages 218-219.
8. Given, J. J., "Hosea," *The Pulpit Commentary*, vol. 13, *Daniel, Hosea, and Joel*, ed. H. D. M. Spence and Joseph S. Exell (Grand Rapids, MI:.Eerdmans, 1950), pages 166-167.
9. Harris, Archer, and Waltke, *Theological Wordbook of the Old Testament*, vol. I, pages 672-673.
10. Tregelles, Samuel P., *Gesenius' Hebrew-Chaldee Lexicon to the Old Testament* (Grand Rapids, MI: Baker Book House, 1979), pages 612-613.
11. Lewin, Roger, "No Dinosaurs This Time," *Science* 221 (1983), page 1169.
12. Raloff, Janet, "Earth Day 1980: The 29th Day?" *Science News* 117 (1980), page 270.
13. Raloff, page 270.
14. Ehrlich, Paul R.; Ehrlich, Anne H.; and Holdren, J. P., *Ecoscience: Population, Resources, Environment* (San Francisco: Freeman, 1977), page 142.
15. Ehrlich, Paul R., and Ehrlich, Anne H., *Extinction: The Causes and Consequences of the Disappearance of Species* (New York: Ballantine, 1981), page 33.
16. Ehrlich and Ehrlich, page 23.
17. Harris, Archer, and Waltke, *Theological Wordbook of the Old Testament*, vol. I, pages 378-379.

Six: Theological Basis for Long Creation Days

1. Harris, R. Laird; Archer, Gleason L.; and Waltke, Bruce K., *Theological Wordbook of the Old Testament*, vol. I (Chicago: Moody, 1980), pages 51-52.
2. Psalm 119:160, Titus 1:2, Hebrews 6:18, *The Holy Bible, New International Version*.
3. Genesis 1:1, Hebrews 11:3, *The Holy Bible, New International Version*.
4. Ross, Hugh, *The Fingerprint of God*, second edition (Orange, CA: Promise Publishing, 1991).
5. Ross, Hugh, *The Creator and the Cosmos* (Colorado Springs, CO: NavPress, 1993).
6. 2 Timothy 3:16, *The Holy Bible, New International Version*.
7. Ross, Hugh, *Biblical Forecasts of Scientific Discoveries* (Pasadena, CA: Reasons To Believe, 1976).
8. Ross, Hugh, *Fulfilled Prophecy: Evidence for the Reliability of the Bible* (Pasadena, CA: Reasons To Believe, 1975).
9. With certainty astrophysicists can conclude that no significant quanti-

ties of matter traveled at faster than light velocities once the universe was older than 10^{-33} seconds. Before 10^{-33} seconds, the possibility exists, but the breadth of the universe during that period of hyperinflation would never exceed the dimensions of a grapefruit.

10. Archer, Gleason L., "A Response to the Trustworthiness of Scripture in Areas Relating to Natural Science," *Hermeneutics, Inerrancy, and the Bible*, ed. Earl D. Radmacher and Robert D. Preus (Grand Rapids, MI: Academie Books, 1986), page 329.

11. Ross, Hugh, *Death: An Extreme Mercy* (Pasadena, CA: Reasons To Believe, 1991); an audiotape with accompanying paper called *God's Mercy in Death*. A two-hour video documentary on the subject will be released in 1994.

12. Ham, Ken, "Billions, Millions, or Thousands—Does It Matter?" *Back to Genesis* 29, (May 1991), page b.

13. Ham, Ken, "Closing the Gap," *Back to Genesis* (February 1990), page c.

14. Zemansky, Mark W., *Heat and Thermodynamics*, fourth edition (New York: McGraw-Hill, 1957), pages 139-194.

15. Ross, Hugh, *The Fingerprint of God*, second edition, pages 44-50, 109-111.

16. Ham, Ken, "Were You There," *Back to Genesis* (October 1989), pages a-c.

17. Ham, Ken, "Be a Berean," *Back to Genesis* 43 (July 1992), page d.

18. Ham, Ken, "Do the Days Really Matter?" *Back to Genesis* 21 (September 1990), pages a, c.

19. Origen, "On First Principles, Book III, Chapter V," *Origen on First Principles*, trans. G. W. Butterworth, introduction by Henri DeLubac (New York: Harper Torchbooks, Harper and Row, 1966), pages 237-242.

20. Ross, *The Fingerprint of God*, pages 172-178.

21. Thayer, Joseph H., *Thayer's Greek-English Lexicon of the New Testament* (Grand Rapids, MI: Baker Book, 1977), page 168.

22. Akridge, Russell, "A Recent Creation Interpretation of the Big Bang and Expanding Universe," *Bible-Science Newsletter* (May 1982), pages 1, 4.

Seven: Do Long Creation Days Imply Evolution?

1. Whitcomb, John C., Jr., and Morris, Henry M., *The Genesis Flood* (Grand Rapids, MI: Baker Book House, 1961), pages 66-69 (in particular figure 4 on page 67 shows, for example, zebras and horses evolving from a single horse kind pair on board Noah's ark), and pages 80-87.

2. Shapiro, Robert, *Origins: A Skeptic's Guide to the Origin of Life on Earth* (New York: Summit Books, 1986), page 128.

3. Ross, Hugh, *The Creator and the Cosmos* (Colorado Springs, CO: NavPress, 1993), pages 141-146.

4. Yockey, Hubert P., *Information Theory and Molecular Biology* (Cambridge, UK: Cambridge University Press, 1992), pages 131-342.

5. Hart, Michael H., "Atmospheric Evolution, the Drake Equation, and DNA: Sparse Life in an Infinite Universe," *Physical Cosmology and Philosophy*, ed. John Leslie (New York: Macmillan, 1990), pages 263-264.

6. Ross, pages 105-121.

7. Ross, pages 137-138.
8. Battson, Arthur L., III, *On the Origin of Stasis by Means of Natural Processes: An Empirical Alternative to the Creation/Evolution Dichotomy* (Colorado Springs, CO: Access Research Network, 1993).
9. On one of our Reasons To Believe television episodes (aired in 1992 on the Trinity Broadcasting Network) I interviewed three research biologists from three different research groups at the California Institute of Technology. After describing how they received Jesus Christ as Lord and Savior and how they became active in the evangelical Christian community, each of them gave an estimate as to how many in each of their research groups of about thirty-five biologists per group would identify themselves as Christians. Their answers: 50 percent, 35 percent, and 25 percent, respectively.

Eight: Do Long Creation Days Imperil Faith and Morality?

1. Miniter, Richard, "Religion Stands Up to Big Brother," *Insight* 7 (June 1993), page 15.
2. Morris, Henry M., "Recent Creation Is a Vital Doctrine," *Impact* 132 (June 1984), page iv.
3. Morris, John, "How Can A Geology Professor Believe That the Earth Is Young?" *Back to Genesis* 29 (May 1991), page d.
4. Morris, John,"How Can A Geology Professor Believe That the Earth Is Young?" page d.
5. Morris, John, "How Can A Geology Professor Believe That the Earth Is Young?" page d.
6. Morris, Henry M., *The Long War Against God* (Grand Rapids, MI: Baker Book House, 1992), pages 105, 134.
7. Morris, John, page d.
8. Morris, Henry M., page 320.
9. Morris, Henry M., page 320.
10. Morris, Henry M., "Recent Creation Is a Vital Doctrine," *Impact* 132 (June 1984), page iii.
11. BSA editors, "Pulse," *Bible Science News*, vol. 30, no. 8 (1992), page 12.
12. Ham, Ken, "What Is a Creationist?" *Back to Genesis* 30 (June 1991), page b.
13. Ham, "What Is a Creationist?" page b.
14. Morris, John, "Why Should a Christian Believe in Creation?" *Back to Genesis* 31 (July 1991), page d.
15. Morris, John, "Evolution and the Wages of Sin," *Impact* 209 (November 1990), pages iii-iv.
16. Ham, Ken, "Billions, Millions, or Thousands—Does It Matter?" *Back to Genesis* 29 (May 1991), page b.
17. BSA editors, page 12.
18. Ham, "Billions, Millions, or Thousands—Does It Matter?" page b.
19. Humphreys, Russell, letter dated 22 January 1992 to Paul Crouch, president of the Trinity Broadcasting Network, copied to me and three

other Christian leaders, pages 1-2.

20. Morris, Henry M., and Morris, John D., *Science, Scripture, and the Young Earth* (El Cajon, CA: Institute for Creation Research, 1989), page 67.

21. Dobson, James C.; Gish, Duane; and Ross, Hugh, "Origins of the Universe," Focus on the Family radio broadcast, August 13 & 14, 1992. The recorded portion of the dialogue was two and a half hours long. A forty-eight-minute edited version is available on audio cassette from Focus on the Family, Colorado Springs, CO 80995.

22. Morris, Henry M., page ii.

Nine: Scientific Evidences for the Universe's Age

1. Sandage, Allan R., et al., "The Cepheid Distance to IC 4182: Calibration of M_V(max) for SN Ia 1937C and the Value of H_o," *Astrophysical Journal Letters* 401 (1992), pages L7-L10.

2. Schwarzschild, Bertram, "Supernova Distance Measurements Suggest an Older, Larger Universe," *Physics Today* (November 1992), pages 17-20.

3. Lindley, David, "A Distant Candle," *Nature* 360 (1992), page 413.

4. Ross, Hugh, *The Creator and the Cosmos* (Colorado Springs, CO: Navpress, 1993), pages 20-27.

5. McClure, Robert D., et al., "CCD Photometry of the Globular Cluster M68," *Astronomical Journal* 93 (1987), pages 1144-1165.

6. Pilachowski, Catherine A., "The Abundance of Oxygen in M92 Giant Stars," *Astrophysical Journal Letters* 326 (1988), pages L57-L60.

7. Hesser, James E., et al., "A CCD Color-Magnitude Study of 47 Tucanae," *Publications of the Astronomical Society of the Pacific* 99 (1987), pages 739-808.

8. Hesser, pages 739-808.

9. Davies, R. E., and Koch, R. H., "All the Observed Universe Has Contributed to Life," *Philosophical Transactions of the Royal Society*, 334B (1991), pages 391-403.

10. Ross, Hugh, *The Fingerprint of God*, second edition (Orange, CA: Promise, 1991), pages 79-84.

11. Cox, John P., and Giuli, Thomas R., *Principles of Stellar Structure, Volume II: Applications To Stars* (New York: Gordon and Breach, 1968), page 979.

12. Norman, Trevor, and Setterfield, Barry, "The Atomic Constants, Light, and Time," *Stanford Research Institute International, Technical Report* (August 1987). This report was published without the permission of SRI International.

13. Goldstein, S. J.; Trasco, J. D.; and Ogburn III, T. J., "On the Velocity of Light Three Centuries Ago, *Astronomical Journal* 78 (1973), pages 122-125.

14. Fackerell, Edward D., "The Age of the Astronomical Universe," *Ex Nihilo Technical Journal*, vol. 1 (1984), pages 90-91.

15. Norman and Setterfield, page 11.

16. Peacock, John, "Fresh Light on Dark Ages," *Nature* 355 (1992), page 203.

17. Uson, J. M.; Bagri, D. S.; and Cornwell, T. J.; *Physical Review Letters* 67 (1991), pages 3328-3331.

18. Lamoreaux, S. K.; Jacobs, J. P.; Heckel, B. R.; Raab, F. J.; and Forston, E. N., "New Limits on Spatial Anisotropy from Optically Pumped ^{201}Hg and ^{199}Hg," *Physical Review Letters* 57 (1986), pages 3125-3128.

19. Slusher, Harold S., *Age of the Cosmos* (Santee, CA: Institute for Creation Research, 1980), pages 33-37.

20. Moon, Parry, and Spencer, Domina Eberle, "Binary Stars and the Velocity of Light," *Journal of the Optical Society of America* 43 (1953), pages 639-645.

21. Fackcrell, page 88.

22. Ross, *The Fingerprint of God*, pages 43-47.

23. Ham, Ken, "Were You There?" *Back to Genesis* (October 1989), page b.

24. Ham, Ken, "Billions, Millions, or Thousands—Does It Matter?" *Back to Genesis* 29 (May 1991), page b.

25. Hammond, Allen, and Margulis, Lynn, "Creationism As Science: Farewell to Newton, Einstein, Darwin . . . ," *Science 81* (December 1981), page 55.

Ten: Is There Scientific Evidence for a Young Universe?

1. Brown, Walter T., *In the Beginning*, fifth edition (Phoenix, AZ: Center for Scientific Creation, 1989), pages 11-19, 45-56, 89-96.

2. Morris, Henry M., "The Young Earth," *Institute for Creation Research Impact Series* 17, ICR Acts & Facts, vol 3, no. 8 (San Diego, September 1974), page i.

3. Blick, Edward F., *A Scientific Analysis of Genesis* (Oklahoma City, OK: Hearthstone Publishing, 1991), pages 81, 97-99.

4. Monastersky, R., "Speedy Spin Kept Early Earth From Freezing," *Science News* 143 (1993), page 373.

5. Pettersson, H., "Cosmic Spherules and Meteoritic Dust," *Scientific American* 202 (February 1960), pages 123-132.

6. Whitcomb, J. C., and DeYoung, D. B., *The Moon: Its Creation, Form, and Significance* (Winona Lake, IN: BMH Books, 1978), pages 94-95.

7. Blick, Edward F., *Special Creation vs. Evolution* (Oklahoma City: Southwest Radio Church, 1981), pages 20-21.

8. Slusher, Harold S., *Age of the Cosmos* (San Diego, CA: Institute for Creation Research, 1980), pages 40-42.

9. Dohnanyi, J. S., "Interplanetary Objects in Review: Statistics of Their Masses and Dynamics," *Icarus* 17 (1972), pages 1-48.

10. Jacobs, J. A.; Russell, R. D.; and Tuzo Wilson, J., *Physics and Geology* (New York: McGraw-Hill, 1959), page 135.

11. LaBonte, Barry, and Howard, Robert, *Science* 214 (1981), pages 907-909.

12. Gentry, Robert V., *Creation's Tiny Mystery* (Knoxville, TN: Earth Science Associates, 1986).

13. Wakefield, Jeffrey Richard, "The Geology of Gentry's 'Tiny Mystery,'" *Journal of Geological Education* 36 (1988), pages 161-175.

14. Wakefield, J. Richard, "Gentry's Tiny Mystery — Unsupported by Geology," in *Creation/Evolution, XXII* (1988), pages 13-33.
15. Odom, A. Leroy, and Rink, William J., "Giant Radiation-Induced Color Halos in Quartz: Solution to a Riddle," *Science* 246 (1989), pages 107-109.
16. Odom and Rink, page 109.
17 Austin, Stephen A., "Mount St. Helens and Catastrophism," *Institute for Creation Research Impact Series* 157 (1986), pages i-iv.
18. Jacobs, Russell, and Tuzo Wilson.
19. Wonderly, Daniel E., *Neglect of Geological Data: Sedimentary Strata Compared with Young-Earth Creationist Writings* (Hatfield, PA: Interdisciplinary Biblical Research Institute, 1987).
20. Phillips, Perry G., *Tidal Slowdown, Coral Growth, and the Age of the Earth* (Hatfield, PA: Interdisciplinary Biblical Research Institute, 1989).
21. Hayward, Alan, *Creation and Evolution: The Facts and the Fallacies* (London, UK: Triangle Books, 1985), pages 95-96.
22. Slusher, pages 15-16. Russell Humphreys, an adjunct professor of physics at the Institute for Creation Research, has raised the same point in a number of radio forums with me.
23. Prendergast, Kevin H., *The Evolution of Galaxy Structures, June Institute Lectures,* Department of Astronomy, University of Toronto (1971). At this week-long intensive course I had the privilege of viewing Prendergast's 16mm films of his models of various classes of galaxies proceeding through all their development phases as well as other films displaying the dynamics of close encounters of galaxies.
24. Cowen, Ron, "Were Spiral Galaxies Once More Common?" *Science News,* vol. 142 (1992), page 390.
25. Cowen, Ron, "Tracking the Evolution of Galaxies," *Science News,* vol. 143 (1993), page 15.
26. Prendergast (1971).
27. Prendergast (1971).
28. Morris, Henry M., and Whitcomb, John C., *The Genesis Flood* (Grand Rapids, MI: Baker Book House, 1961), pages 173-175.
29. Morris, John D., *Tracking Those Incredible Dinosaurs . . . and the People Who Knew Them* (San Diego, CA: Creation-Life Publishers, 1980).
30. Baugh, Carl E., and Wilson, Clifford A., *Dinosaur: Scientific Evidence that Dinosaurs and Men Walked Together* (Orange, CA: Promise, 1987).
31. Neufeld, Berney, "Dinosaur Tracks and Giant Men," *Origins,* vol. 2, no. 2 (1975), pages 64-76.
32. Schadewald, Robert, "Scientific Creationism and Error," *Creation/Evolution,* vol. 6, no. 1 (1986), pages 5-9.
33. Kuban, Glen J., "A Summary of the Taylor Site Evidence," *Creation/Evolution,* vol. 6, no. 1 (1986), pages 10-28.
34. Hastings, Ronnie J., "Tracking Those Incredible Creationists — The Trail Continues," *Creation/Evolution,* vol. 6, no. 1 (1986), pages 19-27.
35. Taylor, Paul S., *Notice Regarding the Motion Picture Footprints in Stone, Form N-6* (Mesa, AZ: Films for Christ Association, 5 December 1985).

36. Morris, John D., "The Paluxy Mystery," *Institute for Creation Research Impact Series* 151 (January 1986), pages i-iv.
37. Slusher, pages 43-54. Russell Humphreys, an adjunct professor of physics at the Institute for Creation Research, has raised the same point in a number of radio forums with me.
38. Dixon, Robert T., *Dynamic Astronomy*, sixth edition (Englewood Cliffs, NJ: Prentise-Hall, 1992), pages 263-264.
39. Quoted by Sarah Boxer, "Will Creationism Rise Again?" *Discover* (October 1987), page 85.
40. Stewart, John, *Bible On The Line*, KKLA radio, North Hollywood, Calif., 6 December 1987.
41. Stewart, John, *John Stewart Live*, KBRT radio, Costa Mesa, Calif., 14 April 1993. The actual comments by John Stewart were made to me during the advertisement breaks.

Eleven: Acceptance of Physical Reality

1. Hummel, Charles E., *The Galileo Connection: Resolving Conflicts Between Science & the Bible* (Downers Grove, IL: InterVarsity, 1986), page 111.
2. Morris, Henry M., *Biblical Cosmology and Modern Science* (Grand Rapids, MI: Baker Book House, 1970), page 60.
3. Brown, Walter T., Jr., *In The Beginning* (Phoenix, AZ: Center For Scientific Creation, 1989), page 110.
4. Morris, Henry M., "The Logic of Biblical Creation," *Impact* (El Cajon, CA: Institute for Creation Research, July 1990), pages i-ii.
5. Whitcomb, John C., Jr., *The Early Earth* (Grand Rapids, MI: Baker Book House, 1972), pages 50, 54-58.
6. Petersen, Dennis R., *Unlocking the Mysteries of Creation, Volume One* (South Lake Tahoe, CA: Christian Equippers International, 1986), page 44.
7. Bird, W. R., *The Origin of Species Revisited: The Theories of Evolution and of Abrupt Appearance*, vol. I (New York: Philosophical Library, 1989), pages 415-417. Though these volumes support a young-universe interpretation, in a recent personal communication, Wendell Bird made it clear that he is not committed to the young-universe cause.

Twelve: Embracing the Greatest Discovery of the Century

1. The discoveries mentioned here are explained and documented in two of my other books, *The Creator and the Cosmos* (Colorado Springs, CO: NavPress, 1993) and *The Fingerprint of God*, second edition (Orange, CA: Promise Publishing, 1991).
2. Greenstein, George, *The Symbiotic Universe: Life and Mind in the Cosmos* (New York: William Morrow, 1988), page 27.
3. Davies, Paul, *God and the New Physics* (New York: Simon and Schuster, 1983), pages viii-ix, 25-57, 228-229.
4. Davies, Paul, *Superforce* (New York: Simon and Schuster, 1984), page 243.

5. Davies, Paul, *The Cosmic Blueprint* (New York: Simon and Schuster, 1988), page 203.

6. Jastrow, Robert, *God and the Astronomers* (New York: W. W. Norton, 1978), page 116.

7. Associated Press, "U.S. Scientists Find a 'Holy Grail': Ripples at Edge of the Universe," *London International Herald Tribune*, Friday, 24 April 1992, page 1.

8. Maugh, Thomas H., II, "Relics of 'Big Bang' Seen for First Time," *Los Angeles Times*, Friday, 24 April 1992, pages A1 and A30.

9. Hawkes, Nigel, "Hunt On for Dark Secret of Universe," *London Times*, Saturday, 25 April 1992, page 1.

10. Hogan, Craig J., "Experimental Triumph," *Nature* 344 (1990), pages 107-108.

11. Ross, *The Creator and the Cosmos*, pages 69-75.

12. Ross, Hugh, "Big Bang Breakthrough: Ripples Reach Headlines," *Facts & Faith* 6 (1992), pages 1-5.

13. Cowen, Ron, "Hubble: A Universe Without End," *Science News*, vol. 141 (1992), page 79.

14. Roberts, David H., et al., "The Hubble Constant from VLA Measurement of the Time Delay in the Double Quasar 0957+561," *Nature* 352 (1991), pages 43-45.

15. Jauncey, D. L., et al., "An Unusually Strong Einstein Ring in the Radio Source PKS 1830-211," *Nature* 352 (1991), pages 132-134.

16. Cowen, Ron, "And a Search for Dark Matter," *Science News*, vol. 141 (1992), page 79.

17. Peterson, I., "Gravity Lenses for Peering into Darkness," *Science News*, vol. 141 (1992), page 293.

18. Loh, Edwin D., and Spillar, Earl J., "A Measurement of the Mass Density of the Universe," *Astrophysical Journal Letters* 307 (1986), pages L1-L4.

19. Cowen, Ron, "Boring into an Ancient Star," *Science News*, vol. 141 (1992), page 79.

20. Pagel, B. E. J., "Beryllium and the Big Bang," *Nature* 354 (1991), pages 267-268.

21. Maugh.

22. Briggs, David, "Science, Religion, Are Discovering Commonality in Big Bang Theory," *Los Angeles Times*, Saturday, 2 May 1992, pages B6-B7.

23. Strauss, Stephen, "An Innocent's Guide to the Big Bang Theory," *The Toronto Globe and Mail*, Saturday, 25 April 1992, page 1.

24. Gish, Duane, "Genesis: A Recent Earth/Recent Man Interpretation" and "Speakers' Panel on Genesis," *Science & Genesis*, lecture series sponsored by The Institute of Apologetics in the Study of Christianity held at Rolling Hills Estates Covenant Church, Rolling Hills Estates, Calif., December 5 and 12, 1988.

25. Gish, Duane, "Big Bang Theory Collapses," *Impact* 216, Institute for Creation Research (June 1991), pages i-iv.

26. Bethe, Hans A., and Critchfield, C. L., *Physical Review* 54 (1938), page

248.

27. Bethe, Hans A., *Physical Review* 55 (1939), page 434.
28. Ross, *The Creator and the Cosmos*, pages 105-135.
29. Ross, Hugh, "Computer Models Reveal New Evidence of God's Care," *Facts & Faith*, vol. 7, no. 3 (1993), pages 1-2.
30. Ross, *The Creator and the Cosmos*.

Thirteen: The Narrow Window of Time

1. Ross, Hugh, *The Creator and the Cosmos* (Colorado Springs, CO: Nav-Press, 1993), pages 124-125.
2. Ross, pages 126-127, 130.
3. Ross, pages 127-128, 130-132.
4. Ross, pages 128-129, 132.
5. Ross, Hugh, "Computer Models Reveal New Evidence of God's Care," *Facts & Faith*, vol. 7, no. 3 (1993), pages 1-3.
6. Ross, *The Creator and the Cosmos*, pages 123-146.
7. In 1 Corinthians 4 Paul indicates that all the angels of heaven appear to have their attention focused on human events on Earth. In Hebrews 10 Christ is said to have made one sacrifice once and for all on one planet.
8. Schwarzschild, Martin, *Structure and Evolution of the Stars* (New York: Dover Publications, 1958), pages 73-74.
9. Cox, John P., and Giuli, Thomas R., *Principles of Stellar Structure, Volume I: Physical Principles* (New York: Gordon and Breach, 1968), pages 487-496.
10. Schwarzschild, page 75.
11. Cox and Giuli, pages 508-523,
12. Cox and Giuli, *Principles of Stellar Structure, Volume II: Applications to Stars*, pages 1007-1024.
13. Ross, *The Creator and the Cosmos*, page 126.
14. Cox and Giuli, *Principles of Stellar Structure, Volume II*, pages 960-977.
15. Cox and Giuli, *Principles of Stellar Structure, Volume II*, pages 977-992.
16. Ross, *The Creator and the Cosmos*, pages 128-129
17. Ross, *The Creator and the Cosmos*, pages 126-128.

Fourteen: Evidence for Divine Craftsmanship

1. Psalm 8:3-4, *The Holy Bible, New International Version*.
2. Ross, Hugh, *The Creator and the Cosmos* (Colorado Springs, CO: Nav-Press, 1993), pages 112, 117-118.
3. Ross, pages 124-125.
4. Bower, Bruce, "Retooled Ancestors," *Science News* 133 (1988), pages 344-345.
5. Bower, Bruce, "Early Human Skeleton Apes Its Ancestors," *Science News* 131 (1987), page 340.
6. Bower, Bruce, "Family Feud: Enter the 'Black Skull,'" *Science News* 131 (1987), pages 58-59.
7. Simon, C., "Stone-Age Sanctuary, Oldest Known Shrine, Discovered in

Spain," *Science News* 120 (1981), page 357.
8. Bower, Bruce, "When the Human Spirit Soared," *Science News* 130 (1986), pages 378-379.
9. Jones, J. S., and Rouhani, S., "Human Evolution: How Small Was the Bottleneck?" *Nature* 319 (1986), pages 449-450.
10. Bower, "Retooled Ancestors," pages 344-345.
11. Bower, "Early Human Skeleton Apes Its Ancestors," page 340.
12. Lewin, Roger, "Unexpected Anatomy in Homo Erectus," *Science* 226 (1984), page 529.

Sixteen: Making Sense of Genesis 1
1. Broderick, James, *Galileo: The Man, His Work, His Misfortunes* (New York: Harper and Row, 1964), pages 75-77.
2. Mansoor, Menahem, *Biblical Hebrew Step by Step*, vol. 1, second edition (Grand Rapids, MI: Baker Book House, 1980), pages 69-70.
3. Mansoor, *Biblical Hebrew Step by Step*, vol. 2, second edition, pages 136-141.
4. Waltke, Bruce, *Creation and Chaos: An Exegetical and Theological Study of Biblical Cosmogony* (Portland, OR: Western Conservative Baptist Seminary, 1974), pages 20, 25-26. As Waltke explained in his Kenneth S. Kantzer Lectures in Systematic Theology given 8-10 January 1991 at Trinity Evangelical Divinity School, Deerfield, Ill., the Hebrew words *shamayim* and *erets* when placed together form a compound word which, like the English compound word *butterfly*, takes on a meaning of its own.
5. Archer, Gleason, communicated to me, Barry Beitzel, Walt Kaiser, Kenneth Kantzer, and Bruce Waltke on 9 January 1991 at Trinity Evangelical Divinity School, Deerfield, Ill.
6. Newman, Robert C., and Eckelmann, Herman, *Genesis One and the Origin of the Earth* (Grand Rapids, MI: Baker Book House, 1977), pages 70-72, 80-81.
7. Ross, Hugh, *Genesis One: A Scientific Perspective,* second edition (Pasadena, CA: Reasons To Believe, 1983).

Seventeen: Attempt at Reconciliation
1. Boice, James Montgomery, *Does Inerrancy Matter?* (Oakland, CA: International Council of Biblical Inerrancy, 1979), page 2.
2. Boice, page 2.
3. Radmacher, Earl D., and Preus, Robert D., ed., *Hermeneutics, Inerrancy, and the Bible, Proceedings from the ICBI Summit II, 1982, in Chicago, IL* (Grand Rapids, MI: Academie Books, 1984), pages 901-903.

Eighteen: New Proposal for Lasting Peace
1. 2 Corinthians 11:23, *The Holy Bible, New International Version.*

Name Index

Subject Index

Author

Hugh Ross earned a B.Sc. in physics from the University of British Columbia and an M.Sc. and Ph.D. in astronomy from the University of Toronto. For several years he continued his research on quasars and galaxies as a post-doctoral fellow at the California Institute of Technology. For eleven years he served as minister of evangelism at Sierra Madre Congregational Church.

Today he directs the efforts of Reasons To Believe, an institute founded to research and proclaim the factual basis for faith in God and in His Word, the Bible. He also hosts a weekly television series called "Reasons To Believe" on the Trinity Broadcasting Network. Over the years Hugh has given several hundred lectures, seminars, and courses, both in the United States and abroad, on Christian apologetics. He lives in Southern California with his wife, Kathy, and sons, Joel and David.

Reasons To Believe

Reasons To Believe is a nonprofit organization, without denominational affiliation, adhering to the doctrinal statements of the National Association of Evangelicals and of the International Council on Biblical Inerrancy. It provides research and teaching on the harmony of God's revelation in the words of the Bible and in the facts of nature. Speakers are available for churches, business clubs, university outreach, etc. A hotline for those with questions or a desire to dialogue on issues pertaining to faith, science, and the Bible operates at (818)335-1480, Monday through Friday, 5-7 p.m., Pacific Time. A catalog of materials may be obtained by phoning the same number during office hours or by writing Reasons To Believe, P. O. Box 5978, Pasadena CA 91117.